LIVING ALONE

Devotions for women who are single again

ARLENE COOK

Publishers Since 1798

THOMAS NELSON PUBLISHERS
Nashville

Published in Nashville, Tennessee, by Thomas Nelson, Inc., Publishers, and distributed in Canada by Word Communications, Ltd., Richmond, British Columbia, and in the United Kingdom by Word (UK), Ltd., Milton Keynes, England.

Unless otherwise noted, Scripture quotations are from the NEW KING JAMES VERSION. Copyright © 1979, 1980, 1982, Thomas Nelson, Inc., Publishers.

Scripture quotations marked KJV are from the KING JAMES VERSION.

Library of Congress Cataloging-in-Publication Data

Cook, Arlene.
    Living alone : devotions for women who are single again / Arlene Cook.
        p.   cm.
    ISBN 0-8407-3473-5
    1. Divorced women—Prayer-books and devotions—English. 2. Widows—Prayer-books and devotions—English. 3. Devotional calendars. I. Title.
BV4596.D58C66   1993
242'.6433—dc20   93-7504
                                              CIP

Printed in the United States of America

1 2 3 4 5 6 7 – 98 97 96 95 94 93

To June Masters Bacher,
my mentor and dear friend

But now abide faith, hope, love, these three;
but the greatest of these is love.
(1 Cor. 13:13)

IN THE BEGINNING

SCRIPTURE FOCUS

Psalm 139:14
Philippians 4:13

I remember the minister saying, "Therefore a man leaves his father and his mother and cleaves to his wife, and they become one flesh." It was the happiest day of my life.

My wedding ceremony was probably much like yours, even though the setting and circumstances were different. You may have married in a parsonage before close family and friends or eloped. Or, you may have walked down a long aisle behind beaming bridesmaids to recite your vows in the presence of a large congregation. That's what I did.

We are alike in other ways. We were brought up to believe that it isn't good for us to live alone and that one day Prince Charming would come along. Then we would be adults with all rights and responsibilities. Our lives would finally begin.

I arrived at the altar fully prepared for a lifetime of commitment, sharing, and intimate caring. I fully accepted God's ordinance in Ephesians 5:23 for the husband to be the head of the wife as Christ is head of the church. I felt truly blessed.

Although I must have heard the minister add, "until death do you part" and "let no man put asunder what God has joined together," I did not consciously acknowledge those passages on my joyous wedding day, nor did I confront either possibility until years later. Then it was too late and I was left alone.

The loss of coupleness-companionship, support, and safe-keeping—and adjusting to the lifestyle of living alone can be more difficult to cope with than the initial loss of a spouse. It can take longer and cost more in emotional energy, while devastating fragile self-esteem in the process.

Too many of us, Christians included, maintain an aloofness toward women who are learning to live alone. We have a distant sympathy for widows and show little regard for divorcees.

How each of us came to be alone *is* important, and repeating our stories to loved ones keeps alive fond memories and helps bury the rest. This is part of healing.

As unwilling and unprepared as we may feel, now is the time to step forward. We must accept this new beginning as an exciting opportunity to become reacquainted with the wondrous me God created and that He fashioned to do His good works.

Before we can accept and love ourselves, before we dare consider ourselves emotionally equipped to reach out in love again, we need to accept God's gift of faith, love, and forgiveness. Join me as I claim God's promise for lifelong happiness—found in the great commandment of Mark 12:30-31—as my personal guide for this new year.

Love the LORD your God with all your heart, with all your soul, with all your mind, and with all your strength. This is the first commandment. And second, like it, is this: "You shall love your neighbor as yourself." There is no other commandment greater than these.

It is time now to meet the New Year head on, confident that each of us can again be the caring, sharing, resourceful, and fulfilled woman that God intends. The abundant Christian life is ours for the asking. God is waiting for us to rediscover the "self" He created in the beginning.

One final note to remember as we step into the New Year: God has a sense of humor. We are well advised to cultivate one also. The glass slipper is broken, shattered by time or stress. Do we smile with Him or sit in the cinders?

PRAYER FOCUS: *Thank you, Lord, for the gift of faith. Remind me daily that I can do all things through You. Guide my single footsteps so that the prints I leave behind will honor Your Word with a new maturity. Amen.*

OUR FIRST STOP– SPRING!

SCRIPTURE FOCUS

Isaiah 41:10
Isaiah 43:1b

The judge banged the gavel and intoned, "Divorce granted." Then he immediately took off his Ben Franklin glasses, leaned back in his chair, and closed his eyes.

"That's it?" Marcie whispered to her attorney.

"Yes," the attorney replied, closing his brief case and standing. "Good luck. We'll talk next week. I have a hearing in five minutes." A moment later, he was gone.

Marcie managed to walk to the parking lot before collapsing in tears. "In my heart, I know I gave my all to our marriage. Why wasn't it enough?"

"Because there is sin in the world," I replied softly. She wasn't listening. I opened my arms and Marcie fell against me, sobbing as if her heart was broken. *As if?* No. It *was* broken!

"Divorce is more than a legal separation," she cried. "When the judge raised that gavel, he might as well have been wielding an ax. He severed my body with one blow. Half of me walked out the other door."

There are so many kinds of loneliness and so many social tonics. But there is only one cure.

As basic as the needs for food, clothing, and shelter are to the body, equally basic is the need to feel significant. To a woman, feeling significant means: someone cares about me; I have a place where I belong; I have something of value to do. Care of one without attention to the others is disastrous!

All sense of temporal significance may be wrenched from us with the sound of a lowering gavel or a closing casket. The loss of a spouse hurts. I know that. All we can do is pray and listen. God knows the heartbreaks and the loneliness. But He does more than listen to our cries. He answers, and his cure is simple and complete.

Listen as God speaks directly to you, a woman learning to live alone:

Fear not, for I am with you;
Be not dismayed, for I am your God.
I will strengthen you,
Yes, I will help you,
I will uphold you with My righteous
   right hand.

(Isa. 41:10)

How are we to acquire the God-directed strength to go forward? We must accept His friendship. He will not fail us. He created us in His image to serve His purpose, and He promises that our sense of aloneness will leave us as we walk closer beside Him through Bible study, prayer, and a close fellowship with those who put their trust in Jesus Christ.

I think of myself as a mature rosebush in the winter season of my life. I am only *temporarily* stripped naked of self-esteem and emotionally vulnerable to the elements.

I am deeply rooted in my love for Jesus Christ and I trust in His promise to strengthen and uphold me.

Not only has He redeemed me, He tells me I belong! "I have called you by your name; You are Mine" (Isa. 43:1b).

God himself is feeding, nurturing, and strengthening me. He is softening my brittleness. My Creator is preparing me to greet the spring of my spiritual life with a new, budding confidence in myself and in what I can accomplish for His glory.

God knows your name, too. I invite you to be my friend and step out with me in faith to walk beside God as we learn to live alone.

Do you know someone else who is alone? Ask her to join us on our journey.

Our first stop—spring!

PRAYER FOCUS: *"Behold, I stand at the door, and knock. If anyone hears My voice, and open the door, I will come in to him"* (Rev. 3:20). Amen.

"Picture this!"

Our minister announced his sermon text, Acts 12:1-11, and began reading.

(As he read, I imagined Sophia of *"Golden Girls"* fame paraphrasing in my ear, saying, "A dark and dank jail cell. Peter is sleeping peacefully, although bound by heavy chains and lying on the cold stone floor between smelly, snoring guards. Because Peter is a high-risk customer, extra sentries stand guard at the locked prison gate.")

Sophia's narration drifted away as I was caught up in Luke's dramatic account. "An angel of the Lord stood by him, and a light shone in the prison; and He struck Peter on the side and raised him up, saying, 'Arise quickly!' And his chains fell off his hands" (Acts 12:7).

Completely absorbed by the events that followed, I thumbed back a chapter or two and read how Peter healed the sick, raised Tabitha from the dead, and dreamed about animals in a tablecloth. The plot escalated into a dramatization more powerful than the most gripping TV mini-series.

Pastor concluded his sermon and asked us to bow with him in prayer. I marked the place and closed my Bible. As I prayed, I felt free of the chains that had bound my perception of Bible reading since Sunday school days. I had thoroughly enjoyed my brief walk through the pages of God's Word. Furthermore, I understood what I had read! Never again would Satan bristle me with friends' comments, such as, "Now that you are alone, it's better to spend Saturday nights reading the Bible than trolling in a bar." (As if I ever would!)

I have discovered several intriguing ways

to approach Scripture. I want to share some that have become my favorites.

Choose an easy-to-read Bible—perhaps one with a thumb index, large print, and a soft, caressable cover. I am most comfortable with a study version that has a small concordance and other helps.

Read the *Forward*. It provides a flavor and guideline that clears the path for pleasure ahead.

Open the Bible at random. Begin reading as if you were reading a chapter in a novella. Read until you are ready to browse through another section of Scripture.

Read the *Introduction* found at the beginning of each book of the Bible. Find out who wrote the book, when, to whom, and its intended purpose.

Check the *marginal notes* at the side of each page. These notes create a fascinating daisy chain that winds through the Bible, linking truths, times, and events.

Glance through the *Concordance* in the back. Trace the use of words, such as *justice* and *ordain*. Trace the lives of dynamic women by reading their biographies. You'll find some interesting ones in Ruth and Esther.

Build a historical time-line by reading the books of the Bible in the order they were written.

Note the Scripture text of your favorite hymn and look it up. Compare the lyrics with the text. Dig deeper into Scripture with the help of Bible dictionaries, handbooks, and study programs. You'll find good selections in Christian bookstores, your own church library, and occasionally, in used bookstores.

The Bible was named the book "that most influenced my life," when the Book-of-the-Month Club recently polled a sampling of members. That's no surprise.

PRAYER FOCUS: *Heavenly Father, guide my walk through Your Word. Open my mind to understanding and my heart to total commitment to the Book-of-Life club. Amen.*

I awakened with a start. Fear was racing through me. Without moving a muscle, I strained to hear a repeat of whatever sound had jerked me from a sound sleep. I was certain someone was testing the lock on a sliding glass door or trying to pry open a downstairs window.

Paralyzed with fear, I waited. All I heard were birds chirping in the pecan tree outside my window. They sang as if they had not a care in the world.

How long was it before I relaxed enough to drift off to sleep? I don't know. It seemed only minutes before the alarm clock began its incessant beeping.

I sat up, tired and groggy. My feet found the floor and I caught sight of my reflection in the full-length mirror across the room. I felt strung out, and I looked wrung out. My defenses were depleted. I had barely survived my first four nights alone. How quickly I had become a slave to Satan's right-hand man—invisible fear.

In a few hours enemy swords would be poised again to rip holes in the night's fragile dreams. I needed help, I needed it immediately!

I reached for my Bible and turned to the Book of Psalms, where David shared my lament.

> But You, O Lord are a shield for me,
> My glory and the One who lifts up my
>   head. . . .
> I will not be afraid of ten thousands
>   of people
> Who have set themselves against me
>   all around. . . .
> Salvation belongs to the Lord.
>   (Ps. 3:3-8)

Closing my eyes, I lifted my voice in prayer. "Father, You know the inner battle waging against me. I trust Your promise to send an angel to encamp around me and deliver me from Satan's grasp" (Ps. 34:7). A sense of peace washed over me and, somehow, I started the day refreshed.

That evening before turning out my light, I opened my Bible and read, "For God has not given us a spirit of fear, but of power and of love and of a sound mind" (2 Tim. 1:7). I was no longer content only to neutralize my fear of night-aloneness. I felt fortified and ready to attack the rest of my invisible fears; many of which are shared by other women who are learning to live alone.

I listed my invisible fears. I included: choking on food, injuring myself in a fall beyond reach of the telephone, becoming suddenly and violently ill, getting an arm, leg, finger, or my head trapped while cleaning or working in the garage, being accosted in a shopping center parking lot, having someone break into my house while I am home, being subjected to a series of obscene telephone calls by one man.

I held up each fear to the light of Scripture and common sense. Two of my fears were outdated. Once I had gotten my arm stuck behind my desk and I know the panic transmitted by a deranged telephone caller. Both incidents occurred while I was married, but alone in the house. Both times God provided an unexpected solution. Neither remedy involved my husband.

If I had choked or fallen sometime during the last thirty-five years, most likely either would have happened while I was alone. A wedding ring was no protection.

> I will call upon the LORD,
>   who is worthy to be praised;
> So shall I be saved from my enemies.
>   (Ps. 18:3)

I fell asleep peacefully, listening to the sound of birds chirping in the pecan tree and thinking, "Look at the birds of the air. Are you not of more value than they?"

Make a list of your fears. Hold them up to

the light of Scripture and your God-given
common sense. Then ask God to destroy your
enemies, and sleep in peace!

PRAYER FOCUS: *"In the multitude of
my anxieties within me, Your comforts
delight my soul" (Ps. 94:19). Amen.*

CHOICES

SCRIPTURE FOCUS

Psalm 68:3
Romans 12:13

We have all heard the adage, "Most people are as happy as they choose to be." It is true, but you and I know that happiness can seem elusive to those of us learning to live alone.

Women alone, too often and always needlessly, share a common bond—loneliness, the lack of intimacy with others.

My friend Beth put it succinctly. "It's one thing to lose a husband," she said. "But I didn't expect to lose my closest couple friends too. I grieve the loss of each of them almost as much as the loss of my husband, because it is willful, unprovoked rejection of me as a person."

She's right. However, the matter was placed in perspective for me when I asked myself, "In all the years I was married, did I *ever* include a woman alone when having a few friends in for dinner, potluck, or dessert?" Never. My invitations were extended to couples whose husbands' interests meshed with those of my husband's. I also thought that women somehow suddenly changed to a different social circle when they were alone. Mostly, I didn't think!

Loneliness is a choice, just as happiness is. So say Christian psychiatrists Frank B. Minirth and Paul D. Meier in their must-read-immediately book, *Happiness Is A Choice*.[1]

After reading this revealing book, I made a conscious decision to ward off loneliness, the forerunner of depression, by keeping my support base intact. And my well-meaning resolve was put to the test within days.

My husband and I belonged to what we referred to affectionately as "the walking group." Seven or eight couples met very early Saturday mornings to stride out on a four-plus mile walk along a hillside trail above

Lake Hodges. The delight of watching for white egrets, jack rabbits, and deer tracks helped relax the mind and regenerate the spirit. Our fellowship concluded with conversation, fresh fruit salad, and cinnamon rolls on Tom and Mary's patio overlooking the lake. That was when I was part of a couple.

After my divorce, I expected a condolence call from Mary. She did call, but I was surprised when she asked, "We will see you Saturday, won't we?"

My forehead suddenly became damp. Feeling strangely light-headed, I sat down at the kitchen table. I knew what my body and my aching heart needed, but if I said yes, could I force myself to drive to their home the following Saturday morning?

I heard God say, "Your life isn't over, it's simply changed!" And I heard myself say, "Yes."

The next step was easier. I invited two couple friends to my home for dessert. The men had one another to talk with and the women weren't bored either. I busied myself hostessing and made a point of not bringing up the subject of my loneliness.

The evening was a success and my guests included me in gatherings they had later in their homes. There are now five to seven of us who gather about once a month in each other's homes for dinner. Sometimes we rent a family-oriented video; sometimes we play a new game; always we have good conversation. The three women have remained my closest friends.

I choose not to be lonely. Believe me, it's worth the effort to be happy!

Make a list of several couples whom you can invite, two at a time, for Sunday evening dessert.

PRAYER FOCUS: *Lord, You have given me the will to choose. I choose happiness. Keep me mindful that lasting happiness is only possible when I cultivate a love relationship with You, myself, and others. Amen.*

GOOD HOUSEKEEPING

SCRIPTURE FOCUS

Psalm 18:2
Psalm 122:7

This is the day of the year when my resolve usually sputters and old habits start eroding my list of well-intended New Year's resolutions.

Not this year. This is the year of new beginnings and of hope born of a realistic evaluation of me as a woman facing the new year living alone.

Unfortunately, you and I live in an old, sinful world. A woman who no longer lives under a man's protective umbrella is vulnerable to all sorts of scams. She is open to emotional and physical attack, even in her own home.

God wants us to have a sense of peace and security in our lives and certainly in our homes. He has given us the ability to help make it happen. We need to be careful not to let it be known we are alone.

Following is a list of ways you can protect your name and address from prying eyes. Doing some or all of these things will make your year more comfortable. You may want to add other changes you need to make. Use this list to help you decide what you need to do.

- Change your telephone number to one that is unlisted or list only your initials and last name without your address.
- Change charge accounts, utility bills, and subscriptions to your initials and last name. Do not put your name on your mailbox. If possible, change your address to a post office box or to your work address.
- Change the heading on your personal checks to reflect your name and post office box or work address, if possible. Have your work number printed on your checks. When asked for an address other than your post office box, give your work address.

- Give your work telephone number when signing a VISA or MasterCharge bill.
- Ask a man to record the outgoing message on your telephone answering machine. Do not give your name or indicate the time of your expected return.
- Keep an old pair of men's work shoes outside the back door. Set a pipe stand or another masculine touch in view of the front door.
- If possible install an electric opener on your garage door.
- If you can afford it, install a fire/burglar security system in your home, which is tied into your local police department via a central station.

Happy New Year! You have earned the good housekeeping seal of approval!

PRAYER FOCUS: *Dear God, shield me from harm with the umbrella of Your protection. Be patient as I learn that "perfect love casts out fear" (1 John 4:18). Amen.*

ROUTINE CHANGES

SCRIPTURE FOCUS

Luke 11:9
2 Corinthians 3:17

T. S. Eliot wrote, "Shall I part my hair behind? Do I dare to eat a peach? . . . I have heard the mermaids singing . . ."[2]

Dare we dream such frivolous thoughts?

Yes! The physical and emotional mega-challenges of our new "Ms." lifestyle demand that we learn to manage stress. A light-hearted change of routine is one of the best and easiest ways to minimize stress overload.

Each of us has a threshold of stress based on personality, self-discipline, and the rules for living imposed by society for our circumstances.

Doing everything the way we have always done is not only a stressful reminder of the way things were, but it can make us feel old and boring, even to ourselves.

My first effort to change a personal ritual was, in retrospect, very small. Then, however, it was a significant change in a thirty year pattern of meal planning. What I did was simple. I went to the grocery store one evening after work and bought a week's worth of weight-conscious microwave dinners!

The first night I sat at the kitchen table and read the evening newspaper while I ate. I didn't feel as alone as usual. The next evening, I watched TV while I dined on lasagna and salad. There were no pots and pans to clean or dishes to do. More importantly, the change in routine distracted me and kept me from dwelling on the fact that I was alone during the only time of day when in the past I was rarely alone.

Next, I decided to take a small step toward changing my routine look. I bought a pair of colored hose to wear with a favorite dress. It was a daring move for me, but the compliments I received the first time I put on the outfit made me feel good!

Routines can be broken in other ways. For example, drive home by a different route, take a bouquet of cut flowers to a shut-in, listen to music while you do your housework. If you wake up in the middle of the night and can't go back to sleep, begin your daily Bible study, work a crossword puzzle, or, as my sister did, teach yourself to play the guitar.

Increasing your level of activity usually helps lower stress. Start with something simple, like taking time to walk through the neighborhood with your eyes open to the variety of plants in bloom, going window shopping, trying a new microwave recipe, or singing aloud while gardening.

Choose something you think will be fun for you. If it isn't, stop it and try something else—without feeling guilty. Probably no single activity will take away all stress, but if you change nothing your stress baggage will certainly hang on and, most likely, get heavier.

You may want to try volunteering. Seeing others with greater problems than your own sometimes puts your life in perspective. More than that though, reaching out to others requires you to interact with them. You may find that you have talents you hadn't discovered that otherwise would have remained hidden.

If your first attempt at changing your routine doesn't give you pleasure and relieve stress, try something different!

PRAYER FOCUS: *Lord, I appreciate the freedom to make changes in my daily routine in order to enjoy Your promise of an abundant life. Guide my choices so that each will honor Your never-changing commitment to my eternal life. Amen.*

HOME ALONE

SCRIPTURE FOCUS

Romans 14:7
2 Timothy 1:7

We were on our way to a city council meeting when I asked Fred why he hadn't stopped by for lunch that day. I asked, "Did you end up having lunch alone?"

"No," he replied. "Life's too short to eat alone."

Fred, seventy-five years old and recently widowed, didn't intend to sound profound. Nevertheless, I found myself thinking about his simple statement of fact. Fred was right. Life is too short to eat alone. Most of us also believe life is too short to shop alone, vacation alone, and sleep alone. What Fred was saying is that those of us who are learning to live alone soon realize *life is too short to spend it being lonely.*

Living alone is not the same as being lonely. Many singles have discovered that living alone can be more than merely tolerable. It can be an enriching experience. Here's how:

- *Live today believing you will always be single.* Don't put off living a full life until you remarry or until a friend invites you to spend an afternoon or a weekend together. Invite a friend to join you at an art exhibit, rodeo, walk-a-thon, hiking weekend, model home tour, or street fair. Treasure new memories rather than dusting a collection of antique regrets.

- *Don't eat alone.* Recognize, as Fred did, that mealtime is an important social event in our culture and eating alone too often can cause emotional indigestion. Loneliness in not confined to one sex. Feel at ease about asking a co-worker, man or woman, to join you for a quick lunch at noon. Weekends can be very long. When they are, plan a Saturday or Sunday night barbecue or pot-luck. Inviting couples will help keep cherished past friendships intact and including a single or two will help ease you into your new lifestyle.

- *Establish a routine.* Stability may seem elusive right now. So look for it in the places you've always found it—a regular Bible study time, a set beauty shop appointment, your morning wake-up time or plant-watering schedule, and in church liturgy.

- *Establish a non-routine.* Is this contradictory? Not really. Living alone sometimes leaves gaps in time that encourage loneliness unless the time is treated as a special blessing. Less rigidity in scheduling chores allows me freedom to enjoy more of my day. For example, I do my laundry-for-one at my convenience. Sometimes it's late at night, but who cares if I spent my usual laundry time doing something else of my choosing? Unschedule and enjoy the time you

spend grocery shopping, bed changing, clothes shopping, bill paying and
you may find time to sneak in an
occasional late-night TV movie.

- *Get a pet.* Pets can be a lot of work!
However, the responsibility of nurturing something other than yourself can
contribute immeasurably to good
mental health. And a dog that barks
when someone nears the door provides valuable security. A cat is a great
companion and can be as indepen-
dent as her mistress. Showing or
breeding animals can bring rich rewards, often forming the basis for
new friendships.

- *Get acquainted with God.* Talk to
Him. I mean talk to God aloud. I have
a friend who sings His praises as she
does her housework and while she
gardens. I don't sing well so I usually
just talk. I haven't changed my address, but I have moved closer to my
Savior. And His zip code never
changes!

PRAYER FOCUS: *Jesus, You know what it feels like to walk alone. I may be single, but I have You. I am never home alone. Amen.*

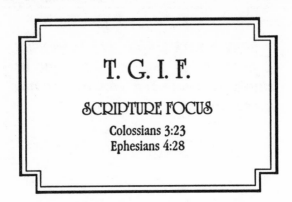

T. G. I. F.

SCRIPTURE FOCUS

Colossians 3:23
Ephesians 4:28

Without saying why, Bonnie asked several friends to gather for a no-hostess luncheon on Saturday at the T.G.I.F. cafe. (T.G.I.F. means, "Thank God It's Friday.")

Bonnie, who was recently divorced after thirty-two years of marriage, waited until all were seated before she announced happily, "I invited you here to help me celebrate my new adventure in living. I am now a career woman. I have completed my first week as a receptionist in a pediatrician's office!"

Charolette laughed, saying, "No wonder none of us crossed your path this week!"

"Congratulations," I offered. "What wise

words do you have to say after five days on the job?"

Bonnie's eyes danced as she raised her water glass in a toast. "T.G.I.F.!" Everyone else raised glasses and repeated her toast, except Rae. During dessert, Rae left the table to go to the ladies lounge. Sensing something was wrong, I followed.

"How's your job hunting going?" I asked casually.

"I can't bring myself to look for work. The idea of punching a time clock at my age is humiliating."

"Why, Rae?"

"It sends a message that the man I loved for twenty-eight years had little respect for his wife, the mother of his children. His first spending priority was his hobby, not a savings or life insurance plan." Tears spilled down her cheeks. "Carl mortgaged everything before he left Bonnie. I don't know how she manages to face any of us!"

"Bonnie understands Economics 101 for a starter. She knows that if she doesn't work, she doesn't eat. She doesn't expect us to judge Carl, and she doesn't expect us to judge her for Carl's behavior. Carl will answer to God for his behavior. Bonnie does need our support. God, the Master Worker, worked to create the world in six days. He ordained work when he put man in the Garden of Eden to work it and take care of it. That is why we are here today—to honor the dignity of work."

Our culture tends to link who we are with what we do. That can be devastating to the already fragile ego of one who is moving into life's fast lane for the first time. Sad, too, is the statistic that at least 25 percent of our workers dislike what they do. Work is often endured in order to receive a paycheck to spend on weekend frolic.

Who can fault Rae for wanting to keep her distance from such a pointless existence? However, after a pep-talk from Bonnie, Rae discovered the solution to satisfaction in the work place lies in focusing on a Christ-honoring attitude.

Paul wrote, "And whatever you do, do it heartily, as to the Lord and not to men" (Col.

3:23). Work not only brings glory to God. When done for Him, it also has moral benefits. Paul tells us that working for ourselves alone is not enough. We must work so we may have something to share with others.

A month later the same group met again at T.G.I.F. This time we were celebrating Rae's first successful week as a Tupperware consultant. Bonnie offered the toast: "Different strokes for different folks."

Do you T.G.I.F. in despair or in hope? Have you checked your attitude lately? Try a T.G.I.M. to start a work week, and remember each of us labors in love for our Savior.

PRAYER FOCUS: *Thank you, Lord, for a nation that allows women the freedom to work for a living wage. I praise You for giving me the freedom to love my labor. Amen.*

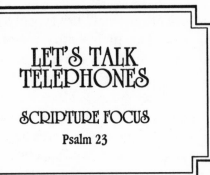

"As a woman alone, which is most important to you—your automatic clothes dryer, panty hose, or a car telephone?"

My friend posed the choices one evening as we drove home along a winding lake-front road after our monthly two-for-one coupon dinner.

I was about to cast my vote for J.C. Penney Control Tops when Sally stopped alongside the road. "Flat tire, I think," she said, climbing out of the car. What now? We were miles from anywhere. What if the wrong kind of person stopped to help? What if no one stopped?

Sally returned and reached for her car

telephone. Twenty minutes later a tow truck had us in his headlights.

The following week I had a phone installed in my car. A frivolous expenditure? No, wise budgeting for the woman living alone, with no one knowing when, or if, she arrives home safely.

One night, I left a meeting at church and was followed by two men in a car. As I drove, I dialed 911 and soon a patrol car responded with flashing lights, pulling over the men's car. I continued on my way with no one knowing I had called for help.

My daughter's home is a three hour drive from mine, much of it across isolated desert. I feel safer making the trip alone, knowing that in case of an emergency, help is within reach.

I've used my car telephone to make and cancel appointments and to let people know I will be late. I've called for more complete directions and have asked friends to turn on porch lights so I could find house numbers. I've reported drunk drivers, accidents, and fires, saving lives and property.

When the phone rings in my car, I know the call is important and cannot be put on hold until I reach my office or home.

I was 30 miles away, driving in another direction, when I received a call that my father had suddenly contracted pneumonia. I immediately changed course and reached his bedside in time to read his favorite Psalms and hymns before God carried him to his heavenly home later that day.

The car telephone is God's unique gift to me and to other women who need a lifeline to protection.

Put a pad and pencil on the front seat of your car. For one month, keep track of the times a car telephone would have served you well.

PRAYER FOCUS: *Dear Lord, only You know the evil that follows me. Fill me with peace that comes from trusting in Your protection. Amen.*

STRESS TEST

SCRIPTURE FOCUS

1 Corinthians 10:13
James 1:12

I was driving to the post office along a quiet residential street. It was a heavenly morning. A recent spring rain had splashed the lush foliage with brightness. Front lawns were cut to velvety richness. The profusion of rainbow blooms, now teased by warm breezes, danced in a lulling sway. I noticed none of it. I was late for a meeting and my stress level was reaching the danger zone.

Just as I entered an intersection, a boy on a bicycle flashed in front of my windshield. I slammed on my brakes and he did too. We came to rest with our frightened eyes a breath apart at the driver's side window.

I reacted with anger. "You could have been killed!"

"Who cares?" he retorted with ten-year-old cockiness, though his dark eyes betrayed pools of hurt. He turned quickly and climbed onto his bike, then disappeared down an alley.

I pulled to the curb and began to sob. I told myself I didn't have time to fall apart. I blindly reached for a notebook that had spilled to the floor, and a loose paper fell into my lap. It was a stress test, compiled by Dr. Richard Rahe of Washington Medical School.[3] I was supposed to fill it out before the meeting, but I hadn't found time.

Let's do it together, now.

How many of these life crises have you experienced in the last six months? Add up your score to find your stress "temperature."

1. Death of a spouse 100
2. Divorce 73
3. Marital separation 65
4. Jail sentence 63
5. Death of a close family member 63
6. Personal injury or illness 53

7. Marriage 50
8. Losing a job 47
9. Marital reconciliation 45
10. Retirement 45
11. Change in health of a family member 44
12. Pregnancy 40
13. Sex difficulties 39
14. Gain of a new family member 39
15. Business readjustment 39
16. Change in financial state 38
17. Death of a close friend 37
18. Change to a different line of work 36
19. More or fewer arguments with a spouse 35
20. High mortgage or loan 31
21. Foreclosure of mortgage or loan 30
22. Change in responsibilities at work 29
23. Son or daughter leaving home 29
24. Trouble with in-laws 29
25. Outstanding personal achievement 28
26. Spouse beginning or stopping work 26
27. Beginning or ending school or college 26
28. Change in living conditions 25
29. Change in personal habits 24

30. Trouble with the boss 23
31. Change in work hours or conditions 20
32. Change in residence 20
33. Change in school or college 20
34. Change in recreation 19
35. Change in church activities 19
36. Change in social activities 18
37. Moderate mortgage or loan 17
38. Change in sleeping habits 16
39. More or fewer family get-togethers 15
40. Change in eating habits 15
41. Vacation 13
42. Christmas 12
43. Minor violation of the law 11

Results: Add up your score.

100 and over: Your stress level has
reached overload. It's time to change
some aspect of your life to reduce
that score.

80–100: You are over-stressed and
your score is reaching the danger
zone. Take steps to learn to relax.

60-80: You are under the average amount of stress.

59 or below: Praise God! Enjoy your stress-free time.

PRAYER FOCUS: *"Now thanks be to God who always leads us in triumph in Christ, and through us diffuses the fragrance of His knowledge in every place" (2 Cor. 2:14). Amen.*

Several friends have asked if I intend to go back to my maiden name. It seems to me that once named, a person acquires a unique and indelible personality. I am what I am.

Names are important and parents for centuries have chosen their children's names because of their meaning. The name I gave my son Jon means "gift of the Lord" in Hebrew. He truly is a gift. My son Alan exemplifies the virtue of harmony, which is the meaning of his name. My name means "pledge." Once I give my word, I am steadfast in keeping it.

God believes in the importance of names. He named Adam "man of earth." Then he gave Adam the privilege of naming Eve, meaning "mother of all living", as well as all the other creatures of the earth. Imagine what a responsibility that must have been!

God spoke through His prophet, Isaiah, to announce that a young woman would bear a son, and He would be called Immanuel, meaning "God with us" (Isa. 7:14). Later, God sent an angel to Mary to inform her that she would bear the Son of the Most High. She was told, "You ... shall call His name JESUS" (Luke 1:31).

God speaks to us through His Word. In Scripture, we find many different names for God's Son, the Savior of all mankind, from which we can draw comfort.

In Hebrews 12:2, Jesus is described as the "author and finisher of our faith." I can't count the number of projects I've started and left unfinished, including the half-knitted sweater in the stand beside my chair. But God finishes everything He starts. He gave me the faith to believe His promise of a Savior. He kept that promise when He was born a babe, endured the cross on Calvary, and died for my sins. He rose from the dead, ascended into heaven, and waits to claim me as His own on judgment day, when His work in me will finally be finished.

Another comforting name for Jesus is found in John 10:9. Jesus says, "I am the door. If anyone enters by Me, he will be saved." Jesus is our portal to peace. In Him I can find safety, joy, and meaning for my life.

One of my favorite references is in The Song of Solomon. This "Song of Songs" is an idyll of love and courtship, described in the highest and purest beauty. It illustrates the relationship between Yahweh and Israel, and between Christ and the church. Song of Solomon 2:1 describes our Savior as, "the rose of Sharon, and the lily of the valleys." This beautiful reference is made only once in the entire Bible.

Although He is a rose by any other name, "Jesus Christ is the same yesterday, today, and forever" (Heb. 13:8). I pledge my faithfulness to Him.

You can find comfort by reminding yourself of Christ's other names upon which you may lean. Look up Isaiah 9:6, Jeremiah 23:6, John 1:14, John 6:51, Hebrews 7:22, and Revelation 19:16.

PRAYER FOCUS: *I love to end my day humming these words of a favorite hymn by John Ellerton[4]:*

Grant us Thy peace upon our homeward way;
With Thee began, with Thee shall end, the day.
Guard Thou the lips from sin, the hearts from shame,
That in this house have called upon Thy name.

Karen opened the trunk and handed out several large packages. Sally, her recently widowed friend, gathered the bundles in her arms and called from behind her mountain of purchases, "Thanks for lunch and for helping me spend my last dollar at Nordstrom's sale!"

"You don't spend money at a sale, you save it!" Karen teased.

"Then come in and help me add up how much I saved. I need all I can scrape together to pay off my credit cards!" Sally's glib response rang a false note in Karen's discerning ears. She followed Sally inside.

Karen had assumed Sally's world was back

in order following Jake's death three months before. But the moment Karen stepped into the den, it was apparent little was in order.

Jake's desk was swamped with an avalanche of unopened mail—about three months worth, Karen guessed. The words, "Final Notice" were stamped in big red letters on several envelopes. Karen turned to face her friend.

Sally burst into tears. "Jake took care of the finances. I didn't know where to begin, so I never did. I've ruined our credit rating forever! I guess I'll have to file bankruptcy, whatever that means."

Sally was indeed in financial trouble. Her plight was almost as serious as Karen's neighbor, Bette.

Bette's husband had converted their assets into cash before leaving town with their bank roll and a younger woman. Bette struggled to maintain her dignity and a normal lifestyle. Unfortunately, she continued to spend for several months as if nothing had happened.

Sadly, these stories of two women left

alone are not unusual. Separation, divorce, and death create a disruption in income that must be addressed. Managing her money is one responsibility single women dare not let slide, yet many do.

You are in financial trouble if you need to borrow money for paying bills. If you have more than one account delinquent for over 120 days, you could be in jeopardy of losing your home or car.

How do you get out of debt *permanently?*

- Admit there is a problem. Ask for God's guidance in setting a difficult course of self-discipline.
- Seek help immediately. The National Foundation for Consumer Credit, Debtors Anonymous, an accountant, or a financial planner can lend a hand. Be prepared to learn budgeting.
- Contact all creditors. Be honest about the situation. Most will be eager to work out a repayment plan that is acceptable.
- Cut up and return credit cards. Cancel all checking overdraft privileges.

- Keep a daily record of *every penny* spent. Analyze all expenses. You may be surprised which expenditures you'll find easy to cut back.
- Create a budget that makes sense, giving the first fruits to God. Expect to make serious lifestyle changes such as moving to less expensive accommodations or renting out a room.
- Tell family and friends of your new resolve. Ask them to uphold you in prayer and to support your cause by not loaning you money in the future.
- Develop a savings goal of three to six months income. Study investment options rather than sale advertisements.

Finally, notice the peace of a fiscal balance. And remember that God's Word is our "final notice." Share His plan of salvation with someone who struggles with the debt of sin.

PRAYER FOCUS: *Father, thank You for the gift of Your Son, Jesus Christ, who died in payment for my sins. Amen.*

DEFINE "VACATION"

SCRIPTURE FOCUS

Psalm 8
Psalm 65:6-13

Bob stuck his head through the doorway and asked, "Do you have summer vacation dates in mind? If not, you might think about it and mark the calendar. The rest of the staff will choose their dates after you."

In my imaginary *Dictionary of Deepest Fears for Women Alone*, the entry for vacation reads: "Vacation, 1. exile. 2. banish." Bob's by-the-way request meant I could no longer postpone the advent of summer. My mind yearned for a change of pace as well as a change of scenery. My fearful heart was the holdout. Surely it was too soon to step from familiar traces and bolt to parts unknown. Celebrating life now would be like dancing on a grave.

During the final years of my marriage, we enjoyed tropical resorts and family camping. Now that I have no family living at home, idling away endless hours on a sandy beach no longer fits my inclinations or bathing suit style.

Just thinking of planning my first travel vacation made me break into a cold sweat. I didn't want to go as a "woman traveling alone." Collecting vacation memories as a single rates zero in my travel diary. Also, being a practical person, I noted the cost of lodging doubles for a single traveler.

I survived by planning my first vacation as a single woman, traveling with a like companion. I prayed for a woman to come with me. One Sunday morning the Lord placed my future vacation roommate in the pew in front of mine. The rest of the story was zany and incredible, and became part of my cherished photo album history!

Most of us who are alone have little time and few leisure dollars to spend. Value is a top priority in selecting a destination. My dream vacation is to experience the "work of His fingers ... everything he put under man's feet," as Psalm 8 describes. Are you my kind of traveler?

Volunteer Vacation: Combine travel with usefulness. Contact your church, or a state or federal natural resources agency. You may wish to assist in building a mission school along the Amazon, dig for fossils, help make maple syrup, record data on humpback whales off Baja, or restore a medieval castle in Germany.

Bonus: volunteer vacations may be tax deductible if the organization is registered with the IRS as a tax-exempt, non-profit corporation.

Educational Vacation: Do you have an unfulfilled passion such as photography, fishing or French cooking? Chances are you can find a workshop or a weekend retreat that will accommodate your deepest desire or indulge your fancy.

If you are more adventurous, a guided tour through the wine country may boost your spirits. No? Then perhaps a whale-watching expedition is more to your taste. Or a week in a covered wagon with cowboy storytelling and singing around a campfire. Carol and I chose to cruise the Mississippi on a lazy excursion back into antebellum days.

Contact travel agencies, colleges, museums, language institutes and zoological societies. All are excellent sources for unusual and rewarding travel vacations throughout God's kingdom.

Bonus: I know several women who serve as hostesses on one-day or week-long bus trips. Some also organize groups for domestic and foreign excursions. Each hostess earns nice discounts or expense-paid trips for her work. Check with your travel agent and local tour companies.

Define the vacation of your dreams. Start planning. Save room for God. He is a world traveler.

Next year's calendar is posted. My vacation dates are inked in and my ticket is reserved. Will you join me?

PRAYER FOCUS: *My mind and heart trust Your loving arms to reach around the world and hold me with Your words, "Lo, I am with you always, even to the end of the age" (Matt. 28:20b). Amen.*

BUTTERFLIES ARE FREE

SCRIPTURE FOCUS

John 8:32
Romans 6:22

Doris, who has lived alone for the last two years, unconsciously twisted her well-worn wedding band around her finger as we talked over the back fence.

"You feel safer with the ring wrapped around your finger?" I asked simply.

She smiled. "Safe, like in a cocoon. I am more self-confident when people think I have a husband in the background to advise and protect me. Besides, I'm not ready to deal with the subject of dating."

I smiled at her defensive reasoning. "Surely you want to remarry. You're a social person, enthusiastic about life. . . ."

"And I love a man's body next to mine in bed."

"Doris!"

"Ask any woman living alone, including any Christian woman, what she misses most about marriage," she countered in a mock whisper. "It's s-e-x. If she's honest, she's either glad to be free and hopes for something better, or she yearns for what she lost. She's still alive, you know."

I shook my head at my gray-haired friend. Doris was delighted to think she startled me with her candidness.

I was startled, although not by her answer. I had once asked my counseling minister what he found to be the most painful common denominator among women who are left alone after a long-term marriage.

He replied easily, "Sexual abandonment, which fosters the loss of self-esteem. A lonely woman is tempted to go into the community in search of a rebound marriage or an illicit affair—both soon regretted."

Doris interrupted my musing. "Another reason I continue to wear my wedding ring is because it makes me feel and act married. I need all the help I can get to resist temptation while I get myself together spiritually and emotionally. I can finally say I am content in Christ and with myself!"

It was Doris' turn to be startled by her own words. She paused, then added, "At this point, I believe I'm wearing my ring out of habit!"

A butterfly was set free.

Like Doris, I'm working on resisting temptation and growing spiritually and emotionally. Some things definitely help, and I call them "Steps Toward Moral Purity For Singles":

Release Tension Through Physical Exercise. Your body is the temple of the Lord. Focus on activities which nurture good health. Garden, join a gym and swim, walk or jog daily, or travel the world from the seat of an exercise bicycle (1 Cor. 6:12–20).

Feed Your Mind A Gourmet Diet. You've heard the saying, "Garbage in, garbage out"? Maintain a Christ-centered attitude by beginning each day in private Bible study and prayer. Enrich your mind by seeing, saying, and listening to God-pleasing music, literature, films, television, and conversation (Phil. 4:8–9).

Travel in Christian Circles. Another adage is "You are known by the company you keep." Choose a mature Christian woman as your best friend, travel companion and confidante. Find someone who understands your needs, and to whom you can look for spiritual strength (Gal. 6:1–2).

Praise God in Your Singleness. Remember the refrigerator magnet that reads, "Be patient, God isn't through with me yet"? Each morning open your heart in praise to the wondrous course God has planned for you. Challenge yourself to close your day by finding a blessing in each event of the day (1 Cor. 7:39–40).

PRAYER FOCUS: *Christ, true God, true Man—You know my longing for loving arms wrapped around me and the loneliness of unwelcome celibacy. I praise You for the promise of power to resist temptation and for the daily reward of joy and peace as I trust in You. Amen.*

MY SOUL REMEMBERS SPRING

SCRIPTURE FOCUS

1 John 5:14
James 5:13-16

"Spring is the handshake of a new friend," writes June Masters Bacher. "A shaft of exploring sun touches the dominant browns of winter with brightness. The woodland, so recently somber-gray, opens one eye while the other dozes. Hickory trees dangle catkins like a headful of emerald curls. Green upon green stretches across the drabness of the marsh. The world takes a deep breath of April air. It is the time of sowing."[5]

No matter what I sow or how I pray, my pen does not yield the rich harvest of word pictures found in June's long-grain poetry. Neither is it likely that prayer will stop my hair from turning silver, nor do I expect prayer to provide permanent world peace.

What good, then, is prayer?

Let's reflect back to the day we chose to strike out together in walking beside God. Did we wonder then how God intended to lead us into the spring of spiritual growth? No, we simply trusted with what little emotional reserve we had left.

God has been, and is true, to His promise. He is strengthening us through His Word and through a close fellowship with Christian friends. And through personal prayer, a conversation with God, we become most intimately acquainted with Jesus Christ, the personage of our strength and support.

It does not take effort to stay on the sideline in a Bible study and let others do the sharing. It is easy to scan the horizon with a broad brush and rob yourself of the depth of God's creation. And life is much less complicated when Christian friends give and you take freely, never getting around to returning hospitality.

Personal prayer is a different matter. From

wherever we seek Him in prayer–in bed, at the dinner table, driving on the highway, or on bended knee in the garden–He immediately tunes in. He listens.

What does He hear? Most of the time He hears us asking for something. Does He always answer? Yes. He may not answer as quickly as we like or in a way we expect. Sometimes His answer may be no.

One of the most exciting aspects of spiritual growth is tuning into God. When I listen with a quiet and open heart, He sometimes tells me why He answers prayer in the way He does. In those moments, I feel the Master's presence. I am Mary, sitting at His feet, learning from Him. These are the special times my soul remembers.

Prayer is more than a Santa Claus relationship with Christ. Prayer is praise. Prayer works best for me when I begin as I would a letter, with a greeting and salutation. To whom do I address my request? To my Savior, Creator, King of Kings, Lord of Lords, Prince of Peace. Is he not also Jesus, the Word, Our Guarantee, and the Door to Life?

When I look at God's credentials, it humbles me. This is what I need to begin prayer—a humble spirit. I listen better to His counsel when my ego isn't in the way.

Sometimes I need to talk to God because I've sinned. Of course, He already knows exactly how I have hurt Him or someone I care about, but confession is good for the soul. Saying I'm sorry to God first makes apologizing to someone else seem easier.

Thank you, Lord, for all blessings great and small. Thank you for the good years of my marriage, for my grandchildren's trust in Jesus. Thank you for today's good health and thank you, God, for inspiring June with the Master's touch.

Thank you, Lord, for spring!

Now it's your turn. List the places you pray. This week add the shower and the grocery check-out line.

PRAYER FOCUS: *"But those who wait on the LORD shall renew their strength"* *(Isa. 40:31a).*

Dottie, dressed in a jumpsuit and wearing large, flashy earrings, breezed past the secretary and popped into my office. "I'm on my way home from the cemetery," she said. "Boy, did I give Charlie a piece of my mind even though it is...was our wedding anniversary."

"Charlie's been dead three years, Dottie. You know he's not in that grave." Charlie had died suddenly in his sleep at age 45.

"I know," she cut in nervously, "he's gone. Still, I go to his grave and talk to him when I get so angry I can't stand it."

"Dottie, you've done a wonderful job taking over the business, managing it and your employees."

She wasn't listening. "I married when I was seventeen. I was Charlie's Dresden doll. He never allowed me to take charge of anything more important than making a hair appointment. The first check I wrote in my life was to the funeral home!"

"He loved you, Dottie. He was only trying to—"

"He also didn't prepare me for last weekend."

"You've lost me, Dottie, what do you mean?"

"I finally sorted through the last box of his personal papers. I discovered there was a time when I wasn't his only doll."

Before I could think of anything comforting to say, Dottie continued, "I know he loved me. I'm just plain angry because ..."

"He's not here to beg your forgiveness, right?" I interjected dramatically.

Dottie grinned broadly, "You've got it!" Then she added, "I don't sound very loving, do I?"

"Love is forgiving. Remember Christ hanging on the cross, totally humiliated and in excruciating pain, calling out in a dying voice, 'Father, forgive them for they know not what they do'? Do we dare do less?"

A long distance call broke into our discussion. Dottie blew me a kiss and darted out. Two weeks later, she reappeared with an invitation to lunch.

"You might think I'm crazy, but I decided I needed to talk to someone other than you and Charlie," she confided over salad. "I went to church and talked to God."

Knowing Dottie, I whispered across the table, "Out loud?"

"Yep. I went to a church that's open all day. I slipped into the back row."

"What happened?"

"The more I talked, the more I sounded like a complaining fishwife. So I quit talking, figuring God knew all about everything anyway, because He's God. Besides, He decided when it was Charlie's time to go, not Charlie. I can't get mad at God."

"How about Charlie?"

She smiled. "I have plenty of cause to be angry with Charlie, and he with me if he could talk back."

Dottie paused and became serious. "I'm the one—not God or Charlie—who's hurt by carrying anger in my heart. What is a wedding anniversary anyway? It's an annual celebration of love and forgiveness. To paraphrase you, do I dare make it less?"

If you have trouble forgiving and forgetting, make a list of specific grievances you hold against your spouse. Pray for power to forgive each transgression. Check off your list until you have shed each ugly burden and are filled with the peace that passes all understanding. Now you are free to remember only the pleasant moments. Happy anniversary!

PRAYER FOCUS: *Heavenly Father, as You forgive me even before I ask, give me the grace to forgive myself and my spouse for his sins against me during our marriage. Amen.*

THE GODLY WOMAN

SCRIPTURE FOCUS

Proverbs 31:25–31
John 15:19

My grandson brought home a Mother's Day card he made in school. Each second grader decorated a card in a unique fashion and independently completed the sentence, "What I like most about my mother is _____." Trevor printed, "She is a Christian."

My daughter was deeply moved. Her goal in life has always been to be a godly woman. What a blessing to have her young son acknowledge and accept God's priority for his mother as his own! The seven year-old's clear thinking comes at a time when confusion reigns throughout the adult world.

Day after day, television commercials and

inane sitcoms attack a woman's self-worth. The media contends that acceptance and success belong exclusively to people who are young, thin, and sexually-oriented.

Our social behavior is dissected, evaluated, and excused according to a checklist of childhood neglects and abuses, from sexual encounters to sugar intake. Our inner strength is measured by our ability to juggle too many responsibilities, assert ourselves in the bedroom and boardroom, and cheerfully accept society's declining values.

You and I do not have the advantage of a husband to guide, direct, and protect us (Gen. 3:16). The world may be going to Hell in a hand basket as Clarice, my widowed friend, believes. Nevertheless, we Christian women have reason to rejoice.

We live *in* the world but we are not *of* the world. In the world, we claim the highest standard of living in the history of womankind. American women are guaranteed equal rights, a privilege unknown to most women in the world.

When we say that we are not of the world,

it means that our Living Lord is our Protector. His Word, which honors and reveres women, is our guide to self-worth, morality and manners. Beginning with Eve, every woman has had the freedom to choose a godly lifestyle.

How godly am I in the Lord's eyes? How godly are you?

A godly woman is tenderhearted, compassionate, patient, and forgiving (Eph. 4:32). She is not foul-mouthed, bitter, quarrelsome, or slanderous—too often the initial behavior of a woman who feels rejected or abandoned by the loss of her husband.

As soon as my friend Clarice unconditionally forgave her husband as Christ forgives each of us, bitterness and anger disappeared. Her broken heart mended and a kinder, gentler spirit blossomed.

A godly woman cherishes her body as a temple of the Holy Spirit (1 Cor. 6:19). Loneliness sometimes overwhelms and smothers a fragile spirit. It can become Satan's crowbar, prying a distraught woman to seek self-worth in illicit sex. Hold fast the vision of Christ hanging on the cross. Hear him cry out in loneliness to his Father. "Why have You forsaken me?" Our isolation pales in comparison.

A godly woman glorifies God with her body. Abstinence is stubbornly considered unbearable in our permissive, AIDS-stricken society. For those of us not of the world, God promises He will never permit more trials than we can bear (1 Cor. 10:13).

Charm is deceitful and beauty is vain. True beauty shines from within. "Lots of gaudy gold and bright colors get a man's attention," insisted my friend Sonya. Then she prayed for wisdom and received it! The Holy Spirit moved in and brought Sonya a prudent attitude and a sense of discretion that honored God (1 Tim. 2:9–10). The spirit of a godly woman is a blessing to all, especially to herself.

PRAYER FOCUS: *Lord, guide me in the way of wisdom that Your eyes may see in me the heart of a godly woman. Amen.*

SCRIPTURE FOCUS

Ruth 1:8–18
Hebrews 13:5b

Insurance company mortality tables indicate that most married women in America will be widowed or divorced sometime in their lives. For every woman left alone there are three families who must adjust: his, her's, and their's.

As unfair as it may seem, when a woman loses a spouse she often loses his family, too. Sometimes she loses them through grief, sometimes through bitterness. Either way, the additional loss of loved ones compounds the heartache.

Josie's husband died of a sudden heart attack while attending a family wedding. He was fifty-five with no medical history of heart trouble. His brothers took charge immediately and remained at Josie's side through the memorial service. Josie, a mother herself, comforted her husband's mother. She loved her mother-in-law and had sat at her kitchen table many times seeking advice and companionship.

Over the next few months, contact between Josie and her husband's family dwindled. Deeply hurt by the rejection, Josie approached her mother-in-law.

"I can barely cope with Steve's death," his mother explained. "You are a painful reminder of his life. Besides, you are young and will marry again. The thought of you dating another man distresses me." The following Christmas Josie and her children were excluded from the family celebration.

Nancy survived an unwanted divorce. She had lost John, her partner, best friend, lover, and the father of her children. She tried to hang onto the remnants of her world by retaining a close relationship with her sister-in-law, a confidante of thirty years. The two usually spent one afternoon a week together.

One day Jenny called. Her tone was definite. "I don't ever want to see you again. John has told me some things about you that are hard to believe. I have to trust what he says. He's my brother and always will be. Our family can't be torn apart by your divorce."

Nancy was devastated. Although she lost Jenny, she and John's mother continued to have a caring relationship. Then, when John's mother died Jenny told Nancy to stay away from the funeral in deference to John.

Women who have walked beside God as they learned to live alone have wise counsel to offer those beginning the long journey. To begin with, stand still. Don't run from grief because it will eventually overtake you. Whether buoyed by family or taking your first steps alone, rely upon God for your strength. His love will sustain you and your heartache will heal, given time.

Pray for and forgive those family members who feel they must choose sides in order to live with themselves. Like Ruth, nurture your relationship with members of your husband's family who still call you daughter, sister, aunt, and friend. Reward their love by recounting only pleasant memories of your marriage and of your former spouse.

PRAYER FOCUS:
Blest be the tie that binds our hearts in Christian love;
The fellowship of kindred minds is like to that above.[6]
>   —*John Fawcett, 1772*
>   *"Blest Be the Tie That Binds"*

It had been a long day, the kind that leaves you tired from the feet up. I was thinking that was exactly what I'd like to do—put my feet up—when the hostess announced dinner.

Angie had called the office late in the afternoon and said, "I'm making chicken and dumplings. How about joining us? There will be six in all." No one of sound mind would turn down one of Angie's home-cooked meals, especially chicken and dumplings!

We gathered around the dining room table and held hands. Another minute or two and I would be answering the call of my growling stomach with a taste of Angie's dumplings.

"Arlene, would you return thanks, please?"

What? My worst fears realized! I was being asked to bless our meal.

Somehow, I stumbled through the next sixty seconds—it seemed like sixty minutes. I tried to thank God for His Son, Jesus Christ, and for the dear friends gathered together. I prayed for protection for our loved ones on vacation and for the food set before us, and for good measure, all the ships at sea!

Mercifully, no one said anything following the group's generous "Amen." A moment later, when everyone else's attention was focused on the food set before us, I was still wondering what happened.

Actually, "what happened" happened a long time ago. And it happened to most of us reared in an era where corporate prayer was a task reserved for the head of the household.

As a child, I was never taught spontaneous, corporate prayer. Instead I memorized prayers like "Come, Lord Jesus, be our guest," and "Now I lay me down to sleep." Prayer time was always preceded by an adult's instruction to "fold your hands, bow your head and close your eyes." Sometime during my teenage

years my father changed the mealtime prayer
format. We listened while he read from a
daily devotional sent out by the church. That
was the extent of our prayer training.

When women of our generation established our own homes, most of us ably trans-
ferred all corporate prayer responsibility to
our husbands, then sons. We skated through
the years.

Now alone, we are in trouble. We are now
heads of household, or one in a group of
women having lunch together, where we
take turns asking the blessing. I no longer
want to feel ill-equipped and uneasy in leading others in prayer. Do you?

There's one simple solution to our problem. All we need to do is follow the prayer
form known as a *collect* found in the front
of most church hymnals. Collects have as
many as five parts: the address, the basis of
the prayer, the petition(s), the purpose, and
the conclusion. These five parts, with some
practice, can serve as a ready outline for use
in formulating a public prayer.

For example: Let's say that a sick friend

asks you to pray with her at her bedside. You might say "Dear Lord and Savior (address), You came to earth that we might have life, and have it more abundantly (basis of prayer), we ask You to restore _____ to health, if it is Your will (petition), so that _____ may soon return home to her family, praising You for Your goodness and mercy (purpose). In Your name we pray (conclusion). Amen."

Not long ago I had the opportunity to ask the blessing at a family potluck. I was not caught unaware and proceeded through my mental outline with confidence. My performance seemed fine until I overheard a not-so-deaf uncle say in a stage whisper,

"Not too bad. Too long, though. But that's a woman!"

He's lucky I didn't include all the ships at sea!

I've learned that long prayers begin with short practice sessions. "Thank you, Lord, for this beautiful day," is a simple way to begin. Why not start today?

PRAYER FOCUS: *"For where two or*

three are gathered together in My name, there am I in the midst of them" (Matt. 18:20 KJV).

Remember the touching scene in *Fiddler On The Roof?* Bespectacled Motel, the local tailor, is showing off his new sewing machine to all the villagers. The Rabbi appears and Motel looks up proudly and asks, "Rabbi, is there a blessing for a sewing machine?" The Rabbi thoughtfully replies, "There is a blessing for everything!"

I wonder if New Testament Christians understand the depth of Motel's request. The ancient blessing was more than a way of asking for God's divine favor. God instructed Moses, Aaron, and his sons to use all-encompassing words when blessing the Israelites:

The LORD bless you and keep you;
The LORD make his face shine upon you,
And be gracious to you;
The LORD lift up His countenance upon you,
    and give you peace.

                        (Num. 6:24–26)

Motel's daily life revolved around his sewing machine. The work he turned out was an extension of his creative personality. A new sewing machine was a sizeable investment, and as we already know, Motel was eager to show off his prized possession.

The five parts of the Rabbi's blessing conveyed hope to Motel that God would:

- Favor and protect his new possession.
- Be pleased by its quality and presentation.
- Be merciful and compassionate when it came to keeping the machine in running order.
- Give approval to what the machine produced.

- Provide a focal point of peace and a
  place of refuge.

Seldom do we have difficulty going to God
in prayer when we have a request or want to
share our troubles. But how often do we
deepen our spiritual life by availing ourselves
of another avenue of prayer—seeking His
blessing?

As surely as love and marriage go together
so does the loss of a spouse necessitate that
a new home be established. Oh, the roof
above may be the same one that sheltered
"us", but now it houses only one. It becomes
an extension of my personality alone.

Motel suddenly found himself at a new
place in life just as we have. His spirit was
right with God when he saw in his new
sewing machine both promise and potential
through God's blessing. We sometimes need
an Old Testament reminder that blessings are
ours today, too, for the asking. We are invited
to ask God to bless our houses!

When we ask God to bless our houses, we
are asking him to:

- Protect our homes from harm and danger from all outside forces.
- Be pleased with the witness of our decorating skills. God does not expect our homes to mirror a Christian bookstore. He does expect that wall hangings, pictures, books, magazines, tapes, CDs, and videos be uplifting to the spirit.
- Keep the repair of our homes worry-free.
- Give approval to what transpires within our homes.
- Provide a place of peace, joy and spiritual refuge by inviting Christ to become the centerpiece of our homes as well as a permanent resident in our hearts.

Ask God to bless your home and your heart with His abiding peace and love.

PRAYER FOCUS: *In my entry hall hangs a cross-stitch sampler. This labor of love was made for me by my honorary daughter, Laura Harris. Thank you,*

Laura. You are another blessing in my life.

"Bless This House"

*Bless this house
O Lord we pray
Make it safe by night and day
Bless these walls so trim and stout
Keeping want and trouble out.
Bless the roof and chimney tall
Let Thy peace lie over all
Bless this door that it may prove
Ever open to joy and love. Amen.*[7]

The wedding party reached the altar. Volume increased with new pomp as the organist played the first bar of Purcell's "Trumpet Tune in D Major." Everyone in the congregation rose. The bride, a delicately veiled illusion, started hesitantly down the rose-strewn aisle toward her intended. Ahead lay a lifelong commitment to love and to cherish.

I felt the tears well up. I shouldn't have come. It was too soon. Then the bride passed by and I was stirred by the scent of orange blossoms, the whisper of rustling taffeta, and her radiant expression. Forty-year-old memories emerged as fresh as the flowers in the bride's bouquet.

When the soloist began to sing "There Will Never Be Another," I quickly dabbed my eyes. I tried to regain my composure by looking at the other guests rather than at the bridal couple kneeling in prayer.

In the row ahead sat Paul, married sixty-seven years and recently widowed. Across the aisle was Barb, not yet fifty years old, who had already lost two husbands in death.

Where are the young people? Then I saw Natalie. Her wheelchair was placed at the end of the row. Behind her, Megan was cuddled next to her grandmother. She lost her parents in an auto accident last year.

Ned Smith placed his arm lovingly around his wife's shoulder. I felt a tug on my heart strings. Then I remembered their heartache. Their only daughter, their dream for a future bride-to-be, ran away when she was fifteen years old.

Across the aisle were the Martins. Next month, she will give birth to a Down's Syndrome baby. And Bob sitting beside me, moved his wife to an Alzheimer's care center recently. She's fifty-eight years old and doesn't know him.

I was not alone. Every person in the sanctuary was familiar with the pain of living in a fallen world.

"Oh God of love, Thou hast established marriage for the welfare and happiness of mankind," Pastor prayed.

Loneliness is not reserved for single people, I thought. Nor is happiness exclusive to marriage. Thank you, Lord, for the years we did have together.

"Bless this husband. May his strength be her protection, his character her boast and pride. Bless this loving wife. Give her that inner beauty of a spirit that never fades. May they not expect that perfection of each other that belongs to Thee. Always, may they see each other through a lover's kind and patient eyes."

There's a rough road ahead. Those of us gathered together know the pitfalls and pain that lie in wait. Still, we had come, offering a Christian family's love and support to this special young couple. We too have experienced God's promises of faithfulness and love. A Christ-centered marriage is the hope of a wonderful journey beyond expectation. So it was. So it will be for them!

"When life is done and the sun is setting, may they be found then as now, still hand in hand, still thanking God for each other. May they serve Thee happily, faithfully, until at last one shall lay the other into the arms of God."

I scanned the sanctuary one more time. How many of these people attended my wedding those many years ago? I counted several. How many times have we laughed, shared, supported and prayed together over the years? We are not all couples, but we are all in God's family. None of us need ever feel alone.

Do you know a couple planning to be married? Include them on your daily prayer list.

PRAYER FOCUS: *"We, being many, are one body in Christ, and individually members of one another"* (Rom. 12:5).

SCRIPTURE FOCUS

Psalm 33:12
Romans 13:1

The phone rang for several minutes. Finally, Doris answered. "I am calling to wish you a Happy Birthday," I said. "Did I interrupt your morning shower?"

"Heavens, no. I was outside putting up my flag. It *is* Flag Day, you know."

I laughed. "That's how I remember your birthday. It's always on Flag Day!"

Doris pointedly asked me, "You haven't put up your flag once since you've been alone, have you?"

How does one explain the awesome sense of responsibility for self that accompanies a woman's sudden aloneness? It takes courage to make decisions alone, sometimes even about small matters. It is less threatening to remain passive than to speak out on important church or community issues.

Hanging out an American flag demands a deep commitment. The red, white and blue snapping in the breeze in the front yard says to the world, "I am not an isolationist. I stand ready to be involved!"

What if the signers of the Declaration of Independence had thought of themselves first and were diverted by the pressure of their personal problems? What if they had wavered in their dedication to the cause of 1776?

Fifty-six patriots, each man knowing well the risks, quilled his signature below the final paragraph of our great charter of freedom. They did not waver.

Those magnificent closing words say, "with a firm reliance on the protection of Divine Providence, we mutually pledge to each other our Lives, our Fortunes and our sacred Honor." Their pledge called for total commitment.

What happened to those fifty-six gallant

men who enabled our first flag to wave? Thomas McKean of Delaware served in Congress without pay while his family remained in hiding and poverty. Delaware claims the top red stripe in our flag.

Among the four honored by New Jersey's red stripe were Richard Stockton and John Hart. Stockton was captured by the enemy and mistreated, his estate ransacked. He died at the age of fifty-one. Hart hid in caves until the war's end. He returned home to find his wife had died and his thirteen children had run for their lives. It is said he died shortly thereafter of a broken heart.

Francis Lewis of New York had his wife imprisoned and his home destroyed. Another red stripe. Thomas Nelson, Jr. of Virginia spent his entire fortune in service to our country. He died penniless and awaits Judgment Day in an unmarked grave. A white stripe for Virginia commemorates his sacrifice.

Others were captured, tortured and murdered. Some died in battle, others lost everything, including family. All kept their pledge.

I, too, have made a pledge. It goes like this: "I pledge allegiance to the flag of the United States of America and to the Republic for which it stands, one nation under God, indivisible, with liberty and justice for all."

Our forefathers, each with firm reliance on God, stepped forward in faith to set in motion what President Lincoln defined as "a government of the people, by the people, for the people."[8]

By God's authority our nation serves as a beacon of freedom to the world. It requires the commitment of every citizen to keep our nation free under God.

Where can we begin? Declare independence. Seek God's alliance in prayer. Fly the flag. Get involved! A woman *can* declare independence. Do you own a flag? If not, buy one. Fly it!

PRAYER FOCUS: *Savior, by Your stripes I am saved. By Your authority I am free to salute the flag with fifty shining stars and thirteen stripes, painted with the blood of men who put You first in their lives. Amen.*

LAUNDRY SACKS AND LAVENDER EYE SHADOW

SCRIPTURE FOCUS

Esther 2:12
Psalm 19:8

Have you ever felt like a laundry sack—plain, utilitarian and dependable? I have.

Does a feeling of feminine inadequacy sometimes rush through your veins like hot liquid, even while you are wearing your best "dry clean only" silk dress?

I thought so.

The cause stems from the sudden acquisition of too much space—in the closet, in the medicine cabinet, and between the bed sheets. And this condition is not exclusive to those of us who are living alone. Many of our sisters, who live with overcrowded closets, overrun medicine cabinets, and unaffectionate bed partners, claim spousal neglect is the culprit. Looking back, some of us may agree.

God is on call twenty-four hours a day via a person-to-person hot line called *prayer*. He offers a cure for every ill. His prescription for my sagging feminine self-esteem was to take a hike, literally.

I closed the front door behind me and started up the drive just as the spring morning sun crested an eastern mountain peak. The countryside, like a giant canvas, came alive with a rosy tint. The tone was the same as the blush in my cosmetic drawer. How long had it been since I had taken time to "put on my face"? A month? Longer? Too long.

The trees along the street, less bare than the last time I noticed, showed a promise of rich new foliage. Deep inside that is how I felt, too—most of the time.

I reached a corner marked by a clump of Nile lilies. The lacy lavender spires danced mischievously. They reminded me of June's eyes dancing when I tell her how lovely she looks wearing lavender eye shadow. June is my mentor and dear friend. She and her husband, George, are also my neighbors.

I turned north and walked until I reached my friend's large rural mailbox. The red flag was up. No doubt another June Masters Bacher manuscript was on its way to the publisher.

I leaned on the mailbox and looked up the cement drive toward their kitchen window. George was making coffee.

I thought about my "Junie Moon"—dependable and always available when I need help with a manuscript. She is utilitarian, too, if that's what organized means. But, plain? Never! June is the epitome of femininity.

George saw me and raised the coffeepot. I waved back.

June lives with constant and excruciating pain throughout her body. Yet when she joins George in the kitchen for their early cup of coffee, her hair is combed, her makeup is applied and her jewelry matches her outfit, even if she's wearing a duster and scuffs.

I remembered the afternoon I took June a bouquet of freshly cut roses from my garden. She was recovering from her most recent surgery. To help her take her mind off her terrible back pain, I asked, "Why are you wearing your heirloom sapphire ring?"

"I feel better on the inside when I make an effort to look pretty on the outside," she confided in a soft voice. It sounded like June understood the subject of laundry sacks.

I was about to continue my walk when I heard George call out from the kitchen window. June was peeking over his shoulder, smiling. "The coffee's ready! How about joining us?" he offered.

"Great! I'll be back in ten minutes." I hurried home, wondering where I'd put my lavender eye shadow.

What feminine "touch" touches you?

PRAYER FOCUS: *Thank you, Lord, for the gift of femininity and for reminding me that I am a better witness when I look and feel my best. Amen.*

WHAT IS A FRIEND

SCRIPTURE FOCUS

Proverbs 18:24
John 15:12–17

"Who is your best friend?" my daughter Alyse asked one day. I was about to answer when she added, "Is it a different person now that you are alone?"

"Let me think about that," I replied, realizing her additional query raised more than one question.

I hold many people in high regard whom I would not affectionately call "friend." What is a friend? A daily confidante? Is a best friend one who wins the prize for longevity in my life? Has my list of friends changed with my single lifestyle? Can a new friend be a best friend?

Proverbs 17:17 defines a friend as one

who "loves at all times." Loyalty is the most treasured quality in a friend. Mutual loyalty is the foundation of friendship. Solomon wisely said in Proverbs 18:24, "A man who has friends must himself be friendly." Am I a friend to my friends?

Most of my childhood friends have grown and moved away. Although we shared the inquisitive years, do early friendships automatically carry life membership? How about high school and college classmates whom I address only through Christmas cards?

Such friends are treasured much like rare books, but are too distant to fulfill the proverb, "a friend in need is a friend indeed." According to Ecclesiastes 4:10, we all need a friend to help us when we fall. "Woe to the man who is alone when he falls/ For he has no one to help him up!"

Certainly "the sweetness of a man's friend gives delight by hearty counsel" (Prov. 27:9). Janie and I have sought each other's advice for thirty-five years, sharing the dramas of real life via 6:00 A.M. telephone exchanges. Busy schedules keep us from meeting more often than for birthday hugs. Nevertheless, we are close in our hearts.

Shirley, Jo Ann, and Angie—wives of cherished couple friendships during my married years. Each continues to include me in her social plans. Their enduring loyalty is priceless to my self-esteem!

However, nothing in this sinful world is perfect, including friendships. The warnings of Jeremiah 9:4-5 bear heeding. When the going gets rough, expect Satan to try and entice weak friends from your side. Expect that he will win a few. Expect to hurt.

Thankfully, God is in charge of my care. He brings new friends into my life before I even know my need. Recently, He brought me Judy. We share little history and no life-changing dramas. Our camaraderie is based on our mutual love for Jesus Christ and our common goal to place Christians into elected office. We work, laugh, and pray together, rejoicing as God weaves miracles around us.

My accumulation of friends is like the body of Christ. Each relationship fills a special need. To lose a friend would be to cut off an important part of my support system.

Jesus, my comforter and my dearest friend, knows my every need. We meet several times a day in prayer—sometimes on the run. He is the source of my strength, supplying friends to satisfy my heart's desire.

Yes, a new friend can be a best friend, especially if it's Jesus! If you don't know Him, get acquainted in prayer and invite Him into your life.

Who listens when you are stressed, defeated? Who shares your triumphs? Who forms the foundation of your social life? What need do you have today? Reach out to a friend. Reach out to Jesus in prayer, and do it now. He's waiting.

PRAYER FOCUS:
What a Friend we have in Jesus,
All our sins and griefs to bear!
What a privilege to carry
Everything to God in prayer![9]
        —Joseph Scriven, 1865
        "What a Friend We Have in Jesus"

She was a quiet soldier in the Old Testament army of the King of Kings. St. Luke wrote little about her. However, his few inspired words pack a powerful message for today's woman who walks alone beside God.

She grew up in Judea, a nation torn by internal strife and corruption. Widowed after seven years of marriage, she spent the next eighty-four years serving her Lord in the temple at Jerusalem. God rewarded her with greater spiritual perception than He bestowed on the religious leaders of her day.

Her name was Anna, the prophetess whose life spanned the entire 1st century.

The shock of her husband's death placed

Anna in the worst possible position as a Jewish woman—a childless widow. The young, vivacious woman could have turned from the Lord in bitterness, agonized over her loss, or spent her days searching for a new husband. Instead, she turned to God for joy and strength, asking Him to meet her needs. She ". . .did not depart from the temple, but served God with fastings and prayers night and day" (Luke 2:37).

Anna's life on the temple grounds was not as serene or as safe as one might expect. Undoubtedly, she attended the Feast of Tabernacles, where Jannaesu, priest-king, showed his contempt for the Pharisees, sparking instant mob violence. God's power must have protected Anna from the ensuing riot that claimed 6,000 lives.

Anna survived one political crises after another, including the often bloody rise and fall of six Judean governments.

Finally, Pompey moved against Jerusalem in the name of Rome, in 65 B.C., and found the temple transformed into a military fortress. It took Pompey three months to break down the temple's thick walls with battering rams.

Can you imagine what Anna's daily life was like during the siege? She was a woman without a man's protection, cloistered for months with thousands of desperate defenders. Could you sleep knowing only the thickness of a crumbling wall stood between you and the conquering Roman army?

When Pompey broke through the walls, he slaughtered the temple priests and 12,000 trapped Jews. He defiled the Holy of Holies. We are not told what atrocities Anna witnessed or suffered.

Was Anna's close walk with God the inspiration that led her broken nation to return to the scriptures and to look for the long-awaited Messiah?

The Jewish people knew Anna by her works. God knew her heart and one day He honored Anna's faithfulness in a unique way. It happened the day Mary and Joseph brought the week-old baby Jesus to the temple to be presented to the Lord, as was the custom.

One of the most moving scenes in the Bible

is of aged Simeon lifting the child Jesus in his arms and crying out,

> For my eyes have seen Your salvation,
> Which You have prepared before the
>   face of all peoples,
> A light to bring revelation to the Gentiles,
> And the glory of Your people Israel.
>
> (Luke 2:30-32)

Anna stood at Simeon's side. The aging prophetess knew she was face-to-face with the Savior of the world, the King of Kings. Her heart pounded with joy as she rushed around the temple grounds sharing the good news. The Messiah has come!

PRAYER FOCUS: *Lord, look into my heart and make me like Anna. May my daily walk be a witness of my faith. May my daughters and my granddaughters follow my footsteps. May our lives be pleasing to You. Amen.*

I bought the "family heirloom" for $10 at the Goodwill in 1956, convinced the best bonding between mother and child happened while rocking—rocking and nursing, rocking and singing, rocking and reading, rocking and nodding to sleep together.

As a single grandmother, I do not consider my grandson Trevor too old to cuddle, even though at age seven his legs hang over the arms of the old cane rocker and dangle half way to the floor.

One day Trevor and I were rocking and talking.

"What do you want to be when you grow

up?" I asked, as if no one had ever asked such an important question before.

"God probably hasn't invented yet what I want to be, Grandma." His impish grin was missing two front teeth. "What does God want you to be?" he asked of me innocently. "You must know because you're already old."

Still rocking, I gave my oldest grandson a squeeze and whispered in his ear, "Jesus promised those who love Him an abundant life. It's up to each of us to decide how to live each day."

Later that night when the house was quiet and the fire was burning low, I drew close to its warmth and took a trip alone in the old rocker. Leisurely, I remembered cherished moments tucked away in those closely-folded hours spent with a child in my arms.

I felt grown up then. However, for me, as for most young mothers, there was no time to ponder the "what do I want to be" question. I was happy being a full-time helpmate and mother.

That was years ago. I am alone now, with an enviable opportunity. I can be whatever I want to be. Am I using it? I stopped rocking and reached for a note pad.

What would I like to do that I'm not doing now? That's easy, I thought. I'd like to follow through on my schedule for daily Bible study and for physical exercise.

How do I use my free time? Am I involved in activities that give me satisfaction? I thought of the Stephen Ministry, a front-line form of Christianity in action that used to take much of my time. Perhaps I should become involved again. Sometime, I'd like to take a course in stained-glass design, and maybe one in cake decorating.

Who are my real friends? Do I see enough of them?

Do I spend too much time with people who make me feel stressed?

Do I like my job? What would I rather do? Are my goals achievable? Am I prepared to make changes or take risks?

Do I like the way I look? Would my zest for life increase with a change in hair style? Does my wardrobe need a breath of fresh accessories?

I leaned back and closed my eyes, considering each question, praying for childlike directness in self-assessment. I know some changes will be more difficult than others. With God's direction, this grandma's going to keep on rockin.'

How would you answer these questions in your life? List the changes you need to make to claim the abundant life Jesus promised. Make your first change today with a smile anticipating the victory to come!

PRAYER FOCUS: *Praise God! I am united with Christ through the everlasting bond of His blood. He is the Rock of my Salvation. Amen.*

It was 5:00 A.M. I awoke to feel a sticky, warm stillness in the air. The heat wave had arrived!

Quickly, I pulled on my work shorts and baggy tee shirt and hurried outside to turn on a few sprinklers. I decided to water my rose bushes by hand before the sun-drenched blooms wilted with the rising temperature.

Have you ever noticed that water cannot be hurried out the end of a garden hose, especially on a summer's morn? It takes a long time to fill the basins because everyone on the street is doing the same thing.

I've come to count my summer watering schedule a blessing. I'm never alone. Spiders dance on lacy webs strung across my path. A garden variety of birds advises the world of my every move. And pulling the hose from bush to bush gives me a close-up view of summer's claim to vibrant reds, rich pinks and cheerful yellows. I marvel at the timing of God's seasons.

Today, the water pressure was lower than usual. I used the extra watering time to examine the profusion of young buds and tender new growth on each rose bush. And I thought of us—you and me.

Remember how we began our walk together, stripped naked of self-esteem and emotionally vulnerable to the elements? Deeply rooted in Christ's promise, we trusted and looked forward to a new spring and a budding confidence in ourselves. Our steps beside Him led to an understanding and commitment to prayer. Prayer strengthened us and our stride became more sure.

Now, among the full-bodied, lavish blooms, I felt another quickening in God's step. "Where am I in my spiritual growth? Have I, too, reached the summer season?" I asked God.

Not surprisingly, He answered by reminding me of a recent sermon on the Beatitudes. I'm always amazed that He knows what I need before I ask Him.

I picked a bouquet of one of my favorite tea roses, First Love. Enjoying the half-open buds, I thought, "Am I willing to live in the world and not be of the world? To give and not be hurt when others only take? To love those who treat me unkindly? To help others without thought of personal gain? To relinquish my rights in order to serve others?"

I carried my harvest of blossoms into the kitchen, remembering the time close friends had an anniversary dinner but did not invite me. They felt their joy would only make my recent loss more difficult for me—and the seating would be uneven.

Katherine brags about her forty-year marriage and ridicules anyone God has not blessed likewise. I suffered her comment in silence. However, it was her husband who bruised my heart with the offer of an illicit affair to assuage *my* loneliness!

Can I rise above the pettiness of the world

and be Christ-like in my attitude toward others?

Not alone, I can't.

The world pressures me to strive for personal independence, happiness at any cost, power, strength without feeling, and deception to reach personal goals. The rewards are self-serving and temporary at best.

I'm not able to dismiss a hurt or hold my tongue 100 percent of the time. Neither can anyone else. But God is teaching me to forgive myself and go on.

Christ expects me to show meekness, righteousness, mercy, a pure heart, and the qualities of a peacemaker. Then I am truly blessed, given hope and joy and the kingdom of heaven as His reward.

I placed the beautiful bouquet in the center of my kitchen table. First Love—Christ is my first love.

Welcome to summer!

PRAYER FOCUS: *"Rejoicing in hope, patient in tribulation, continuing steadfastly in prayer" (Rom. 12:12).*

The guide led us through a small corridor and into a spacious suite of rooms called the queen's bath. Two inside walls were faced with gypsum slabs and frescos of frolicking dolphins. The two outside walls formed a floor-to-ceiling open-air frame for the stunning view of the Isle of Crete far below.

The queens who tarried in these rooms 1200 years before Christ, enjoyed the same panorama. They were pampered with running-water toilets that drained to the sea, rainwater baths, and relaxing body massages.

The remains of precious objects and jars decorated with lotus blossoms were found hidden behind a wooden door. Their quality spoke of beauty treatments as luxurious as those at any famous modern day spa.

It took us another hour to complete the tour of Knossos, the Palace of Minos. While other tourists gave their undivided attention to the magnificence of the throne room and grand staircase, my mind remained focused on the personal pampering of ancient Queen Megaron.

I was envious!

That evening, back aboard ship, I fell asleep talking to God about my silly feelings. I woke up thinking about something Oswald Chambers wrote before I was born. In *My Utmost for His Highest*, he wrote, "It is not so true that 'prayer changes things', as that prayer changes *me* and I change things."[10]

I have been told more than once that I inherited the ungarnished German lifestyle. If I did not treat myself like a queen it was my own fault!

When the ship's boutique opened, I was waiting. "Scented bath powder, please," I said. Suddenly, for less than ten dollars, I felt as coddled as any ancient queen.

We've heard a zillion times that "Beauty is only skin deep." What we fail to remember is that God made skin, too. It's part of the temple we are supposed to care for lovingly. Indulging ourselves doesn't necessarily mean that we are destined to become vain fools and cast aside all Christian values for a bottle of perfumed lotion.

On the contrary, God's Word tells us "Ointment and perfume delight the heart" (Prov. 27:9a), and " . . . the fragrance of your name is ointment poured forth" (Song 1:3). In Esther 2:8–9, future Queen Esther pleased the king and was immediately provided with beauty treatments. David put on lotions before going into the house of the Lord to worship.

I know that I have inner beauty because I am created in His image. It's my outer beauty I've neglected, not so much because I no longer have a man to preen for, but because I have allowed myself to believe that pampering will sidetrack a serious Christian woman. What nonsense!

Nothing puts the lid on hectic days and

revives a tired spirit or a tired body faster than personal pampering. The Lord knows our needs.

From "Herb Lover's Garden," in a recent issue of *Victoria*, I learned that with a few herbs, boiling water, and a cucumber or two, I can create my own hand soak, skin toner, facial steam, and face mask.[11] What fun!

And as a royal treat to myself, I occasionally indulge in an almond oil body massage in my own home just before bedtime.

I traveled half way around the world to discover that the home I've loved for twenty-five years is a palace fit for a queen!

Why don't you share a beauty secret with a friend.

PRAYER FOCUS: *Lord, bless me with ". . . the incorruptible beauty of a gentle and quiet spirit. . .", befitting a daughter of the King of Kings (1 Peter 3:4b).*

Once alone, I felt the need to belong, to draw closer to my family.

When I was very young, I overheard my aunts talking in whispered tones. Listening, I discovered the conversation was about cousins I didn't know existed! How many, what their names were, or where they lived seemed mysteries even to my aunts.

When I grew older, I dared to ask my father about the lost loved ones.

He told me that soon after his parents emigrated to America in 1903, his father, Julius, sent for a younger brother and his family. Another brother remained in Germany.

One day, harsh words between my grandfather and his brother sent the younger one
to settle somewhere north under an altered
family name. That was eighty years ago. The
brothers died, still estranged.

My father and grandmother returned to
East Germany in 1930 for a brief visit with
Julius' remaining family. Later, the bombs of
WW II severed all contact between the fami-
lies, and sixty years of silence followed.

I began a love-search for my generation of
second cousins. My cousin, Bill, shared my
passion for genealogy, but, his extensive dig-
ging among German church records and my
exhaustive U.S. research left us empty-
handed. Disappointed, we committed our lost
cousins to God's keeping. We would have to
wait on heaven for a family reunion.

I'm convinced God loves perfect timing.
One day last summer, He sent an outspoken
Christian, Congressman Bill Dannemeyer, to
address the local Rotary Club. My minister,
who knew of my fruitless search for my lost
cousins, attended and heard the congressman say, "I know this town. My grandfather

was brought here from Germany by his brother, Julius, the local tailor."

My minister quickly cornered the congressman following his speech. Dannemeyer looked at him, unbelieving. That evening over the telephone, the grandchildren of two warring brothers were reunited in joy. We scheduled a family picnic.

Before we could gather for our celebration, I received an unusual telephone call, though it should have come as no surprise.

Dr. Homa Golchin, a Persian living in Germany, was in the area attending her own family reunion. Before Homa left Germany for San Diego, her neighbor had asked her to check the San Diego county directory for his family's unusual surname. Perhaps someone would know the whereabouts of the descendants of those who visited his ancestors in 1930.

Homa found my widowed mother on the first try. Within minutes, she and I were talking on the telephone. We met and became more than God's link uniting two families who were oceans apart. We became friends.

Too soon, Homa returned to her adopted

homeland and her anxiously waiting neighbor. She carried back not only news of the American branch of our family tree, she carried the affection of a new friend.

The Dannemeyer clan came to the annual family picnic, held on the church grounds of the congregation founded by Julius and his wife seventy-five years ago.

Bill and I stood before eighty happily reunited loved ones and announced that within two weeks we ourselves would fly to Germany to visit our cousins, thus completing our family reunion—in His time.

You too can trust God's timing. Write down a problem you are unable to solve. Commit your heart's desire to God's keeping. Save space to record the unexpected way in which God responds—*in His time*.

PRAYER FOCUS: *Thank you, Father of all, for the gifts of a yearning heart and a searching spirit. Thank you for the family of believers who will be reunited by Your blood in the kingdom of heaven. Amen.*

MY GOD IS EVERYWHERE

SCRIPTURE FOCUS

Jeremiah 16:19
Psalm 48:10

Dr. Homa Golchin, a strikingly beautiful Persian Muslim, had been chosen by God to be the instrument of His desire in reuniting me and my cousin Ralf. Our grandfathers had become estranged eighty years ago.

I was eager to be reunited with Homa in her adopted country, Germany, and to meet Ralf, his wife, Ursula, and their family for the first time.

However, the most unforgettable moment of my visit to the old country, came while touring Mindon's famous cathedral. It was there that God's hand-picked messenger posed a question that unexpectedly reunited me with an old, unresolved pain.

Ursula, Homa, and I had hurried up the steep stone steps to the centuries-old cathedral door. We paused at the threshold to admire the ancient stained glass, magnificently carved stone, and breathtaking arched ceiling.

Ursula crossed herself and slipped into a pew to pray. Homa moved silently to a bank of candles. She lighted one and placed it among others before kneeling to meditate in the flower-filled alcove. I stood quietly at the back, watching. I was raised to believe true Christians do not defile God by worshipping with anyone who does not believe exactly as we do.

When we left the cathedral, Homa slipped her arm through mine. Together we retraced our steps down the stone stairs to the marketplace.

"I was surprised to see you, a Muslim, lighting a candle in a Roman Catholic church," I remarked casually.

Homa stopped short and turned to me. I will always remember the look of deep hurt in her dark eyes. My voice caught. I felt a sense of déjà vu of some painful affront I had seen before, somewhere.

Homa, with her Persian-German accent answered in English, "My God is everywhere. Isn't yours?"

"Of course," was my feeble response. I was disappointed in myself and worse, I sensed I had disappointed God.

A week later, on the flight home, I rested my head back on the pillow and consciously journeyed into my past, searching for a memory of those hauntingly sad eyes, and found it. They belonged to me.

My eyes had reflected Homa's same inner confusion when my pastor refused to let me play the lead in our school production of *Joan of Arc.* I was near confirmation and promoting another denomination's doctrine through play-acting was a poor witness, he had insisted. Yet secretly, I had thanked God for giving me, at age twelve, the courage to accept a public witnessing opportunity!

My plane touched down on home soil. By then, I was ready to lay aside the excess baggage of past human error.

My God is everywhere! He is within me wherever I am, wherever I travel. In the future, I will witness to His strength and power over the devil and all false gods by bowing before Him in their presence and I will walk beside Him wherever He leads.

Are you carrying excess baggage that separates you from a close walk with God? Lighten your load and don't look back. Focus on an eternal reunion with Him in heaven. Invite others to walk with you!

PRAYER FOCUS: *"Sing to the LORD a new song, and His praise from the ends of the earth" (Isa. 42:10a).*

HOTEL MAJESTIC

SCRIPTURE FOCUS

Psalm 50:15
Nahum 1:7

Sometimes you don't have to be physically alone to feel alone. I'm certain Joan felt the same as I did when Bill pulled off the high-speed boulevard that ringed Milan, Italy's central district and announced with frustrated finality, "I'm dropping you here. I can't spare another minute. The Duomo is one mile south."

We hurriedly climbed out of the car as Bill called out to his wife, "Call Pucci and explain about the fog, road construction and accidents between here and Torino. I'm already two hours late for our meeting!"

"Where and when do we meet you?" I asked.

"The train station. There are hotels all

around it. Let's say 7:00 P.M., on the mezzanine of...the Hotel Majestic. We'll drive back to Torino from there."

A moment later we were left standing in an isolated industrial area, on the far side of a fast track around Milan.

Joan suddenly spotted a rare, signaled crosswalk fifty feet back. Our apprehension turned to giddiness with a green light. We sensed God's control.

We hurried across the street and stepped into an oasis—an unexpected mini-row of retail stores. The first was a quaint bookstore. The proprietor understood us and marked our route to Milan's cathedral. She explained the intricacies of using *The Underground*, priceless information in a foreign city. Next door was a restaurant where we made Bill's call, used a clean restroom and ordered lunch in English. The last shop in the row was a beauty salon. (God sees our every need and so did the hairdresser.)

An hour later, freshly coiffured, we struck out on our walking tour of Milan's antiquities.

At 5:30 P.M. we bought our subway tickets

at the newsstand. Minutes later, we were standing on the steps of Central Station in the deepening twilight, scanning the dozen lighted signs across the piazza for the name of our rendezvous hotel. There was no Hotel Majestic!

Neither the polizi, Hertz, nor taxi drivers recognized the hotel's name. We found Tourist Information on the second floor of Central Station. A listing of Milan hotels revealed a Diana Majestic, located 15 minutes away. What a long-shot!

We took a taxi to the Diana Majestic, sat down in a lobby without a mezzanine and waited. Our heavenly tourist guide would have to provide a way for Bill to find us in a city of six million Italian-speaking people.

The desk clerk suggested that Bill might be found at the Excelsior, a hotel across from the railroad station that closely resembled the Diana. He had Bill paged, but there was no reply.

Shortly after 7:00 P.M., the lobby phone rang, sending a green light flashing through my mind. Joan and I looked knowingly at one another. It was Bill, calling from the Excelsior mezzanine.

Later, Bill explained that while he pictured the Excelsior, he thought its name was Hotel Majestic—until he saw the gold lettering on the facade. Near panic, he asked the desk clerk if any hotel in Milan had "majestic" in its name. He had never been to the Diana Majestic to know the exteriors of the two hotels were similar.

It was after midnight when we arrived at our hotel, The Genio, near the train station in Torino. Before that moment, none of us could have seen the bright green neon sign across the boulevard blazing—Hotel Majestic.

Count the times in this story you see God's hand at work. Do you recognize His hand in your life?

PRAYER FOCUS: *Lord, remind me each day that You are my guide along familiar paths as well as our green light into unknown adventures. Teach me to trust Your sense of direction.*

TERROR IN THE TUNNEL

SCRIPTURE FOCUS

Psalm 56:3
Psalm 94:22

Italian drivers are wild. Ask anyone who has survived travel in "the boot." Italians believe one-way streets are private parking lots, sidewalks are for jay-driving, and red and green signals are year-round Christmas decorations.

On the autobahn, Italian drivers cut, slice, and straddle lane lines with the speed of an electric salami slicer.

Our German car rental company insisted we exchange our BMW for a less expensive rental before crossing into Italy. We prearranged a swap in Freidrichshofen. When we arrived, we found the agency closed for the day. A storm was pushing at our backs. Eight hours of Alps driving lay ahead. We thanked God for arranging an extension on the BMW.

We tried again in Nice, France, to exchange vehicles. Strangely, none were available. Fog and darkness were creeping closer. At our own insurance risk, we elected to press on to our next stop—Torino, Italy.

A mountainous ridge rises from the sea along the Riviera from Nice to Genoa. The autobahn weaves a decorative double chain of hundreds of tunnels and bridges between ports.

Traffic raced across the bridges, piercing the gray thickness at one hundred miles per hour. The tunnels sparkled with reflected ceiling lights bouncing off high-density moving color. The stress of irresponsible speed tightened every muscle in our bodies.

We entered a half-mile long tunnel and rounded a blind curve. Suddenly ahead, a wall of red taillights flashed danger. Traffic was stopped dead as far as the eye could see!

Bill pumped the breaks, hard. I glanced out the rear window. The driver behind slowed with us. We stopped. He stopped. The next six vehicles did not.

I still hear screeching tires, ripping metal and shattering glass repeated five times over—again and again as the sound of each collision ricocheted off the tunnel walls and echoed helter-skelter.

I waited for the whoosh of a fiery explosion from behind that would claim us all. Only steam rose, hissing and sputtering from a serpentine tangle of twisted steel that counted at least six vehicles demolished. Our uninsured vehicle was undamaged and we were unhurt. We praised God, again, for His protection.

Many stalled drivers ahead passed the time in conversation at the tunnel's entrance. Ambulances (mostly unneeded) and tow trucks eventually cleared the tangled mess behind us.

An hour later, traffic ahead started to move. Frantic drivers ran to their vehicles and revved their engines. The double chain moved, then picked up speed.

Almost too late, Bill saw a driverless vehicle

still parked in the tunnel's fast lane and swerved around it. As we passed, I caught sight of a woman sitting in the front passenger seat, her face pressed against the side window. Our eyes met and her look of absolute terror tore through me. Her companion had to be trapped now outside the tunnel, unable to cross the oncoming traffic to reach their vehicle.

A second later, we were on the bridge, building speed in the fog. There was no way to help. I could only pray, trusting her fate, like ours, to God's protection.

Think of a situation in which you found yourself seemingly without solution. In what unexpected way did God answer prayer?

PRAYER FOCUS: *Lord, I can't orchestrate events or the actions of others to provide me with peace of mind. Only You can provide the peace that passes all understanding. Amen.*

THE SWINGER

SCRIPTURE FOCUS

Ephesians 6:2
Revelation 3:19

You and I belong to the swing generation. Our children still need us, thank heaven, and so do our aging parents, who are living longer due to advances in medical science.

Sometimes our dance cards become overcrowded and we twirl ourselves into a "pity party." It can happen.

I was in the computer room late one afternoon. The printer was spewing out reports and the fax machine was a-hum with incoming messages. I heard the telephone ring above the din.

Although I strained to hear the words, I'll never forget the sound of that frighteningly faint voice. It belonged to my widowed mother.

"What's the matter, Mom?" I asked, alarmed. She was calling from her winter mobile home one hundred miles away.

"I fell on the kitchen floor. I think I broke my leg just above the plastic knee joint. I managed to pull myself within reach of the telephone cord." Mom's resourcefulness was nothing new. "You've called for help?" I asked.

"Yes. Georgianna's coach is a few feet away. She'll be here in a minute and call 911. I might pass out before I could give directions," she added. I remained in telephone contact with my incredible eighty-year-old mother until the ambulance arrived to transport her to a Palm Springs hospital—and alleviate her excruciating pain. I expected a sense of relief. Instead, I felt trapped and angry.

I tried to bring my feelings into focus during the two-hour drive down the narrow Pines to Palms highway to Desert Hospital. I was grief-stricken. I am Mom's primary caregiver and I was not there to oversee her care or to offer comfort. At the same time, frustration raged through me. A quick slip had stripped away Mom's short-lived independence—maybe forever. With her independence went mine. It isn't fair! Why did God let this happen?

True, it isn't fair. God allows bad things to happen to good people because sin rules the world. None of us can escape sin, the cause of suffering and death (Rom. 3:23). Unexplained suffering is often due to the fallen world we live in.

Some sin is personal. Many of us bring pain upon ourselves by choosing to run red lights, eat fattening foods or wear slippers without gripper soles (Ps. 107:17).

Sometimes God uses sin to chasten us and lead us to a better life. Adversity builds character, preparing us for other situations where we are challenged to grow (2 Cor. 12:9).

Nearing the hospital, I took a deep breath and found myself once again at peace. I praised God that Mom had only broken a leg, not her neck. And she had forgiven herself for her own slipper folly, funneling all her energy toward recovery.

I hurried into the emergency room to Mom's side. She was drawn and pale. Her first words were, "Get me a reservation at Redwood Terrace (our church's residential care facility). I want to entertain my friends in style."

I felt the chastening sting. True independence means accepting the challenge to stretch, bend, and swing to a new rhythm.

Think of the last bad thing that happened to you. Was your suffering caused by general sin, personal sin, or God's chastening? Or was it a little of each?

PRAYER FOCUS:
"Search me, O God, and know my heart;
Try me, and know my anxieties;
And see if there is any wicked way in me,
And lead me in the way everlasting."
(Ps. 139:23–24)

BY LETTERS BOUND

SCRIPTURE FOCUS

2 Thessalonians 2:15
2 Corinthians 3:3

Please, may I ask you to give me a letter instead of a gift?
—Playwright John Masefield

I love to write to you—it gives my heart a holiday...
—Emily Dickinson

The first time I noticed Marti as an individual was early one morning as I hurried along the arcade toward the teachers' lounge. I caught a glimpse of our newest staff member in the middle of the school lawn. She was moving on all fours, her nose parting the blades of grass, her rear wagging behind.

"What on earth?" I exclaimed, running

toward her and praying that our first busload of arriving students was stalled somewhere down the road.

"'What on earth' is what I am trying to find out," she replied laughing, and like a giraffe, gracefully unfolded herself and rose to her full six-foot height. Then I noticed the pad and pencil in her hand.

"Ever write haiku?" she asked. I shook my head and she continued. "Strict rules. Basically, three lines, seventeen syllables in all, mirroring a happening in nature. The third line carries a surprise double meaning."

A week later our sixth grade classes were competing in a haiku contest. A year later, free-spirited Marti and her backpack were buzzing around the island of Majorca on a moped. We bound our deepening friendship by our common commitment to reach beyond ourselves. Letters flew back and forth between us, and we chose to write solely in verse!

Eventually, Marti ended her wandering and settled on the far side of the Rockies. Nevertheless, over the past quarter of a

century, we have managed a half-dozen
stanza-length holidays together: During our
brief visits, each of us has committed to
trusting the other to plan surprise reach-out
experiences.

Because I trusted my poetic friend, I have
experienced an exhilarating evening usher-
ing at the Denver Symphony, enjoyed a veg-
etarian soup cooking lesson, overcome
measurable fear during a scuba diving lesson,
stretched my endurance in cross-county skiing, and accepted the challenge to take down-
hill ski lessons at age forty-two!

Nevertheless, once I became single again
my self-confidence took a nosedive and I
found it took considerable inner strength
simply to reach out with an occasional bread-
and-butter note, let alone offer a worthy
contribution to our common commitment.

My friend must have had her ear to the
ground for a second time, as she penned me
a note. Marti reminded me that Emily Dickinson prayed in a letter to a childhood friend:
"Lord, keep all our memories green, and help
on our affection, and tie 'the link that doth

us bind' in a tight bow-knot that will keep it from separation."[12]

I pray you have a friend so dear. Do not allow the circumstances of the moment to close an heirloom album of shared experiences and genuine love.

Declare a holiday! Sit down and write a letter to a friend whom you have neglected for too long. Reach out and draw on your shared memories to build a bridge over loneliness toward a treasured tomorrow.

PRAYER FOCUS: *Lord, thank You for the inheritance of Your letters of inspiration and instruction bound in Your Word. Strengthen my commitment to trust You for inner strength and peace. Free my spirit to reach out to new experiences through Your love. Amen.*

SOLAR CELEBRATION

SCRIPTURE FOCUS

Isaiah 45:6
Psalm 71:17–18

The older I get, the more I seem to resist change. I don't mind the crow's feet marching across my face; I do mind losing the agility to do as much as I did in former seasons. Living alone, I *must* be able to climb, bend, reach and carry an extra measure.

Looking back, it amuses me how cleverly God dealt with my struggle with "age adjustment." He began by putting me in the right place at the right time, which in itself is a gift.

It was the day of the autumnal equinox, the sun's last hurrah, and the last day of long light. I was with friends, winding our way up the black-ribboned highway toward the 10,000 foot elevation of Mt. Holly Resort in southern Utah. Vibrant scarlets, golds and oranges mantled the ridges and splashed down the canyons.

I quickly slipped vanity into my pocket and withdrew my glasses. The view was breathtaking. Individual leaves changed color against a backdrop of quaking aspen, peeling bark deepened to a velvety richness, deer grazed near the forest's hemline.

Later, we settled in my friends' condo, stocked the wood stove with the evening's firewood, and took our chairs out onto a balcony. We overlooked a mountain face carved with barren ski runs. In a couple of months, I thought, when the sun moves farther south and snow covers the mountains, we'll sit here and watch an avalanche of skiers sprinkled like confetti on a snow cone—schuss, slalom and slide down nature's frozen topping.

I remember the first time I challenged the face of the mountain, and how proud I was of my courage when I actually pushed off the precipice. It was exhilarating, being part of the fluid beauty of brightly dressed skiers skiing down the icy slopes in a serpentine chain. At that moment of recall, I admitted to myself that I was content to have physically daring firsts behind me. The more I thought about it, the happier I was that I no longer had to turn the soil for my spring garden, climb the fruit trees to harvest apricots and peaches, or wash windows for the holidays. I have arrived, I thought. Let someone younger do it!

From my view on the deck, I realized that this afternoon of the equinox presented a fresh excitement all its own. There was a peace that hung in the mountain air, thin and dried to an autumn crispness. Even the stillness, punctuated by the dropping of a tired pine cone or the tapping of a busy woodpecker, did not disturb the spirit of God's message.

Let this year's solar celebration remind me that God is in His heaven. He guides the sun along its path as He guides each of us through the seasons of life. Each season offers unique challenges and satisfying rewards. It doesn't take rose-colored glasses or maturity to appreciate God's goodness in change.

PRAYER FOCUS: *Lord, only You remain a constant in my life. Only You carry me from sunrise to sunrise, through every season, every change in life. Remind me, daily, that You are the Son, the Light of my world and I am never alone. Amen.*

Mom deftly played the last two cards in her hand. "Count up!" she laughed.

I was left holding a handful of cards, including two twenty-point aces. I still have a thing or two to learn from my mother.

I was dealing another hand on Mom's bed sheet in pre-operative when a tall figure dressed in hospital greens pushed aside the curtain. "The operating suite is ready, ladies." Dr. Knutson's dark eyes twinkled above his surgical mask at the card craziness spread thither and yon.

After a hug and silent prayer, the entourage in green moved Mom on her gurney down the hall toward the set of double doors.

I heard Mom giggle at a nurse's clever quip as the swinging doors closed behind her and her band of angels.

I returned to the family waiting room and joined Aunt Bertha. "How are Leona's spirits?" she asked.

"Great." I replied, dropping wearily down beside her. "Already she has the surgical team wound around her little finger. I don't know how she remains so good-natured. I wouldn't be as good a patient if I were going into my second complicated surgery within three months on that broken leg."

"Surgery wouldn't bother me as much as the prospect of another three months on my back in the health center," replied my favorite aunt.

"She's the darling of Redwood Terrace. The nurses love to take care of her." Then I asked thoughtfully, "What makes someone a good patient?"

Aunt Bert smiled softly and whispered knowingly, "Peace of mind."

We decided to take time during the long wait to write "A Patient's Prescription for

Peace of Mind," as a get-well gift to our own patient.

- *Trust the Master Healer.* Surrender your life to His guidance and He will provide a remedy to every painful perplexity in life. You are never alone. Christ the comforter takes twenty-four-hour nursing shifts with no days off.

- *Find strength in hope.* Christ, who suffered on the cross, knows your every infirmity. When darkness seems to surround you, look heavenward to the light that comes from above. Know that His grace is sufficient to brighten your day. Ask Him to send angel companions to lift your spirits. He'll do it.

- *Breathe out gratitude and praise.* Nothing tends to nurture healing of body and soul more than expressing gratitude and praise. Lavish both on caregivers and loved ones, especially on those who do not treat you tenderly.

- *Praise God.* Open your heart to the Son-light of His presence. Thank Him for His daily dose of blessings, from a wrinkle-free bed sheet to an unexpected visitor. Focus on His love, not on your imperfections. Turn your thoughts away from yourself, giving inner healing room to grow.

- *Give happiness to others.* Giving is one of the best medicines for a diseased body or mind. A good deed goes down easily and leaves a satisfying taste! Minister from your bed by listening attentively to the needs of a friend on the telephone. Offer light-hearted encouragement to a tired caregiver. Give a bedside visitor the comfort of an understanding touch.

The next day we presented the "prescription" to our somewhat groggy patient. Mom scanned our list and sighed, "I'm nice to everyone because

I'm defenseless. I need everyone to *want* to take good care of me!"

A minute later, Mom drifted off to sleep with a peaceful smile on her face. I won't tell her she snores, if you won't!

PRAYER FOCUS: *"In everything give thanks; for this is the will of God in Christ Jesus for you"* (1 Thes. 5:18).

IN LYDIA'S FOOTSTEPS

SCRIPTURE FOCUS

Ecclesiastes 11:6
Acts 16:14-15

When the pavement changed to hand-laid red brick, I knew I had reached the heart of middle America. It looked much the same as it had fifty years ago. My heartbeat quickened as I turned onto Third Street and scanned the row of houses, in search of the white cottage with the peaked roof and manicured rose-bush garden.

I spotted my destination a half-block away. It wasn't the freshly painted green shutters that caught my attention. It was the white sign swinging lazily in the Kansas breeze that read, "Monograms and Personalized Embroidery by Nadine." What began as a hobby had become a serious business for my friend following her husband's death three years before.

Nadine's involvement in a cottage industry is not unique. It is estimated that twenty-five percent of this country's work force earn extra or full-time income from businesses operating out of living rooms, garages and kitchens across America.

As I settled later in Nadine's guest room, I found the bedspread folded back and a monogrammed purple nightgown waiting on my pillow. I felt like royalty and hurried to the kitchen to thank my modern-day Lydia.

Curious, I asked Nadine, "You are set, financially. Why tie yourself to a home business?"

In the blink of an eye she replied, "I must keep busy or I would be lonesome and unhappy. My business brings me company. If not for customers, I could go days without seeing anyone. I couldn't handle that!"

Nadine doesn't feel chained to work. She loves to travel. She often unhooks the sign, puts it in the house and locks the door as she leaves for the airport.

I don't know how many of the 26 million

work-at-home Americans are women learning to live alone. Fran began by selling home-grown vegetables from her garden. Now she leases enough farmland to supply two fresh produce stands located at busy intersections. Karen buys flowers wholesale and stores them in a commercial refrigerator on the porch. She does the floral arrangements for weddings.

The first year Susan was alone, she worked ten months making things for a Christmas boutique. She sold out in one day at her first "Winter Festival," held in her home. She currently employs twelve women. They work all year in their homes, creating a wide variety of holiday decorations to sell at her expanded home sale.

Many of our sisters-in-faith operate beauty shops, mail order businesses, and secretarial and bookkeeping services in their homes. Others work as self-employed consultants for companies like Amway and Mary Kay.

Many of us trying to enter or reenter the work force feel defeated and frustrated by our lack of recent experience or skills with today's high-tech office equipment.

Working in your home allows a flexible schedule. You may opt to set aside time to catch up with today's technology by attending "user-friendly" instruction classes on the computer and word processor.

In addition, there are at least four innovative national programs designed to help people over fifty-five step into the high-tech age.

Write to: AARP, Worker Equity Dept., 601 NW, Washington, DC 20049; National Displaced Homemakers Network, 1411 K St., NW, Suite 930, Washington, DC 20005; National Council of Aging, 409 Third St., SW, Washington DC 20024; and, EPA Workforce Development, RD-675, 401 M St., SW, Washington, DC 20460.

I thought of Nadine and smiled. Maybe that was a *yellow* brick road leading to her door. The monogramming machine in her shop is ultra high-tech. Things in Kansas are not the way they were fifty years ago!

PRAYER FOCUS: " . . . *the LORD your God will bless you in all your produce and in all the work of your hands, so that you surely rejoice" (Deut. 16:15).*

Squinting against the sun, I scanned the gathering of people milling around the outdoor buffet. Finally, I spotted my friend Lauren sitting on the low patio wall with our host. They were looking down the bank.

As I approached them, Lauren saw me and greeted me with a broad smile. "Jake and I were discussing his lush green ice plant. What's your secret, Jake?"

"The secret," he whispered, pulling us into a huddle, "is water and fertilizer." He winked at us, then excused himself to greet other guests.

I was delighted to have a few minutes with Lauren, a successful stockbroker who thrives

on making daily decisions involving millions
of dollars. "How did your pension fund presentation go Tuesday?" I asked.

"Very well and the room was filled." She
looked pleased. Then she surprised me by
confiding a bit sheepishly, "You'll probably
think I'm crazy, but I accomplished something this morning that gave me much more
satisfaction."

"You closed a global deal?"

"No," she laughed. "I cleaned out the first
twenty feet of junk stored along the wall in
my garage!"

"Lauren, you are a nut! Why are you so
excited?"

"Because I am no longer a slave to the sin
of procrastination! Ron was at my side from
the time I was nineteen until last spring. I
counted on him to pick up the responsibilities
I ignored. Since he's been gone, I've suffered
weighty consequences and missed out on a
few rewards because of my procrastination.
I felt a heavy millstone of failure around my
neck."

"Your life is anything but a failure, Lauren."

"Money? Prestige? Neither buys a lasting sense of worth. Taking control over sin, even in little things, is real power."

"What's your secret? How did you rid yourself of your bad habit?" I thought of the thorn in my flesh.

Lauren considered my question then replied, "Jake actually gave us the answer for healthy growth—food and water. I opened my Bible and God's Word fed me. What I read was a reminder that I could do all things through Him. I prayed for control over my secret sin. I realized I could approach procrastination as I would any business opportunity."

Lauren asked herself what steps she would need to take in order to assure success in business or in life. She developed a simple plan:

- *Get Information.* What do you need to acquire to do the job? In this case, it wasn't data, it was trash bags, boxes, marking pens and the AmVet pick-up phone number.

- *Set A Realistic Goal.* Determine the length of the project, then set mini-goals. Giving two hours a weekend for three weekends is a project completion goal that may be more workable than trying to complete it all at once.
- *Make A Plan.* Lauren gave her sons a week to claim old Cub Scout projects and broken bike frames. Then she began plowing through the rest of the junk, determined to meet her goal. Her plan included team work and a realistic schedule, and the plan worked.

"I've untied the millstone and I'm celebrating freedom!," Lauren declared.

"Congratulations, Lauren! I'm proud of you, too." I smiled from my heart, knowing the freedom Lauren experienced is a taste of the freedom awaiting those of us who trust God. Through His Word and wisdom, God helped Lauren develop a practical plan for a problem in her life. He's just as concerned about our daily frustrations and difficulties as He is about our eternal destiny.

The plan I want to follow is God's plan—it lasts an eternity!

What millstone burdens you today? Ask God to show you how to rid yourself of it forever.

PRAYER FOCUS: *"Therefore you shall be perfect, just as your Father in heaven is perfect" (Matt. 5:48)* .

Have you noticed? A sort of gentleness sets in as summer yields to fall. The distant hills are aloof, cloaked in a patchwork quilt of changing oranges, reds, jeweled burgundies, plums and rich golds. The atmosphere is spiced with quince. Persimmons and pomegranates hang heavy, awaiting harvest. The sunshine has more substance, as if it were melted down. An indefinable sense of satisfaction mellows the world with a shawl of loveliness as if draped affectionately around the shoulder of a friend. Autumn is the season of Christian maturity and shared fruitfulness.

Someone asked me the other day, "Where are you in your spiritual growth?"

"Compared to what? To whom?" We are unique personalities, each dependent on God's grace for our spiritual growth. Nevertheless, it was a fair question. And perhaps it is time for us to consider our Christian maturity. Has God matured us sufficiently to reach out and harvest souls for Him?

Do we understand the gift of salvation through Jesus Christ as our personal Savior? Have we allowed His Word to shape our lives and mold the fruits of our labor? Do our thoughts, words and deeds reflect a witness of footsteps walking beside Christ? Do we seek the fellowship of Christian friends, both men and women?

Church boards and committees desperately need the input of mature members. More and more, women are sought for leadership in administrative roles within the congregation. There are numerous service-oriented organizations in the community looking for women concerned with the needs of others.

Are we willing to reach out with the trust of Lois and Eunice and share the Good News with family and friends, even in the next generation? W.R. Wallace's truism is as old as the Scriptures, "The hand that rocks the cradle is the hand that rules the world." Our influence could light the way for another Timothy. Are we armed with the confidence and courage of a Lydia? She was a wealthy, influential business woman who risked everything by publicly identifying herself with Christ and the Christian community. I pray that we are.

Are we willing to conduct business, figure income tax returns, and write checks for our tithe, offering, and missionary commitment as if God were peeking over our shoulders? He knows our hearts.

Has our Bible study time been fruitful to the point that we are as prepared as Priscilla to teach others, rather than remaining fledgling students? Let's try.

Our Sunday schools cry out for disciples of Christ to sit in His place and allow the little children to come to Him. Perhaps we would prefer to ease into a commitment of spiritual sharing by opening our homes to visiting missionaries or group Bible studies.

Do our personal lives reflect a Dorcus personality? Do we, like Dorcus, have an enormous impact on the community, always doing good for others? Would our volunteering spirit be so missed that Christ would raise us from the dead?

God spoon-fed our quaking hearts into the spring of spiritual growth. He brought us to the full-bloom of summer through His tender teaching of the Beatitudes. Have we reached the autumn of perfection in Him?

Reach out and tell someone. The fields are white with harvest!

What are the ways in which you have grown spiritually since summertime?

PRAYER FOCUS:
May ev'ry mountain height,
Each vale and forest green,
Shine in Thy Word's pure light
And its rich fruits be seen![13]
—Francis S. Key, 1832
"Before the Lord We Bow"

Remember sitting on the front steps after school, waiting for the bus to return to pick up its second load? Perhaps you, too, played games to make the time go by faster. One of our favorites was "Pass It On."

It was a simple game. One person whispered a sentence or two in the next person's ear. The person hearing the story passed it to the next until the last in the group shared the message aloud. The distortion was usually hilarious, especially to eight-year-olds.

I never minded waiting for the late bus since the social time with my friends seemed important. I also liked arriving home near dusk. There was always a light in the window, the smell of dinner in the oven, and a welcoming hug from my mother. Sometimes, I felt sorry for those who had to take the early bus. Their greetings were vacant windows, cold ovens and mothers busy with afternoon chores.

Later, I discovered that the spirit of welcome, comfort and care which had claimed my heart, had a name—hospitality. A gift to share.

"Be hospitable to one another without grumbling" (1 Peter 4:9) Peter told us. "Be kindly affectionate to one another ... distributing to the needs of the saints, given to hospitality" (Rom. 12:10, 13), wrote Paul.

Hospitality differs from social entertaining, where the spotlight is on the hostess's preparation. In contrast, hospitality focuses primarily on the guest's needs, whether for a place to stay, a filling meal, or a listening ear. If you practice hospitality, you cannot be too busy, too tired or too poor to respond to a knock on the door.

While the world hungers to be transformed by the spirit of caring, compassion, and comfort, hospitality appears to be a lost art. What can a woman living alone do to obey God's command to "give preference to one another"? Plenty!

Opening our hearts and our homes affords us the perfect showcase for our feminine heritage of creative expression in decorating, cooking and conversation.

Here are a few ways our homes may say hello:

- Put out a welcome mat that says so, mount a plaque or cross-stitch that asks God's blessing, hang a cinnamon-stick rope in the kitchen.
- A home that says "Welcome," may have: a bowl of fresh fruit on the counter, a bouquet of garden flowers on the table, and wooden utensils in a jar near the stove.
- Aromas that rejuvenate a weary traveler: the smell of crockpot stew in it's sixth hour, rain-scented potpourri in the bathroom, and simmering spiced cider on the kitchen stove. Praise God for autumn!

- Touches that make a visitor feel special: lighted candles clustered anywhere, pictorial books stacked on the coffee table, and a Bible by the bedside.
- Gifts that touch: homemade jam, Bible-verse refrigerator magnets, and monogrammed guest towels.

The sweetness of hospitality is taught, not caught. We can help revive the beauty and joy of sharing our femininity with younger women in an abundance of creative ways.

Begin with an invitation to a tea party, delivered to the neighborhood's young ladies, ages eight to twelve. Punch tastes best in bone china. Cookies have a special flavor taken warm from the oven. Let young hands help.

Invite your pastor and family for dessert. Use your gifts as both a "Mary" and a "Martha" to bless and to learn.

Make your bridal shower gift an afternoon with you in your home. Share your secrets of hospitality and those for making a smooth white sauce, flaky pie crusts, and "real" mashed potatoes.

Hospitality is a secret from the heart. Pass it on!

PRAYER FOCUS:
"She extends her hand to the poor,
Yes, she reaches out her hands to the
needy.
Her children rise up and call her
blessed" (Prov. 31:20, 28a).

It was dusk. The weekly Farmers' Market on Grand Avenue was in full swing. The evening of nostalgia boasted prizewinning beefsteak tomatoes, freshly-baked pies and homemade crafts. The event was the city's latest scheme to entice mall shoppers back to the old retail business district.

Margaret and I finished our sidewalk supper. She was a close friend who had Alzheimer's disease. Just going out for dinner and an evening walk was a challenge for her.

We started toward the parking lot behind the dry cleaning business my grandfather had established in 1911. Suddenly, Margaret pointed upward and exclaimed, "Look, the moon is . . . f . . . full!"

I glanced up, surprised. A huge pale moon had silently risen above the purple peaks of the distant foothills. Its unexpected, over-whelming presence had caused Margaret to forget for a moment that she could not complete a sentence.

An autumn chill washed over me. How long had it been since I dared confront a full moon? It's association with love and romance brought a painful feeling I wanted to avoid. For all its shimmering beauty and special glory, the moon is best loved as the celestial watchman of romance. It can reflect shadowy memories of two hearts drawn close under lacy boughs of a garden willow, or lovers entwined in each others arms on a moonlit beach.

The moment I had dreaded passed with less pain than the long anticipation that preceded it. I was free to share the wonder that Margaret felt but could not express.

Our fathers had played together as chil-dren on Main Street. The same moon that was shining down on us now, shone down on them as they romped among the dancing shadows in autumn's long twilight seventy-five years ago.

Without words, we took comfort in the brilliant moon that has moved with splendor across the heavens for generations. We found peace in this shining beacon of love, and of God's eternal promise on our children, grandchildren and all the heirs of heaven, until eternity.

Alzheimer's disease is the fourth leading cause of death in America. It is usually an illness of the elderly, but may appear in middle age. It is a long-term illness that places a tremendous drain on family finances as care is not covered by private health insurance or Medicare.

Family caregivers are often called the greatest victims of Alzheimer's disease. To learn more about Alzheimer's disease and available family support groups, contact: ADRDA, P.O. Box 5675, Chicago, IL 60680-5675. Or call ADRDA's 24-hour, toll-free hotline: 1-800-621-0379.

Do you know someone in your church or neighborhood who is caring for an Alzheimer's patient? Offer the gift of time. Could you spend an hour a week relieving the wearied caregiver? God bless you!

PRAYER FOCUS: *None of us can bring back the past. Our memories, often bittersweet, are blessedly temporal. Look forward to each rising moon as a reminder to live daily with new wonderment. Release the past and trust the future to God's watchful care.*

My son-in-law Steve says I am too generous with my gifts. My answer is always, "I'm just feathering my nest. When I'm old and feeble, I know where I'll be welcome to come live."

Last Christmas, my son Alan overheard my comment and looked stunned. "It never occurred to me, Mom, that you would ever be old and feeble. I've imagined that you may someday retire and live with Carleen and me. But my picture of your state of life is different."

"How different?" I questioned, tentatively.

Alan grinned. "I picture waking up in the morning and finding a note on the kitchen table. 'Waxed car and pruned roses. Back after a five-mile walk. Fresh-squeezed orange juice in the fridge. Love, Mom.'"

Bribing a son-in-law is not adequate pre-retirement planning; neither is trying to outpace my kids the best way to keep me in morning orange juice.

Most of us believe that pre-retirement planning means a forced savings plan, beginning early in one's career. The assumption is that when you stop working there will be ample funds, (added to social security), to make it 'til the end—if you live frugally.

Don't count on social security alone. Now is the time to learn about annuities, IRA's and other income plans. Also, working part-time can assist in closing the income gap and help keep you from rusting away.

Pre-retirement planning is much more than financial consideration. Attitudes, lifestyle, health, and education, along with finances, will affect how we live out possibly *one-third* of our life span.

Attitude affects retirement planning the most. Those who can't admit they are getting older or view retirement as the *end* of a fruitful life, probably will arrive there unprepared.

Those who look ahead to retirement as an exciting step forward in life, know that a fulfilling retirement isn't something that just happens. It takes pre-planning with a few dreams added.

The way we manage our time now will have an impact on our lives ten to fifteen years from now. Avocations, community involvement, and the church work we do now, will serve us well in the future when the need to feel needed grows stronger.

A recent and exciting medical affirmation states that although old age may slow our reflexes and deplete our strength, aging does not necessarily diminish our mental capacity. Indeed, "oldsters" who play cards and work crossword puzzles use fewer brain cells with greater efficiency than some people half their age.

We should pre-plan to use a lifetime of acquired skills and talents in new and different ways within our home, church and community. The time to do that is now.

Retirement is the time to enroll in the

continuing education classes we missed through the years. Cake decorating? How to reinvest retirement assets? Pottery making? There is something for everyone!

We can't expect retirement to be all play and no work. That's no fun. If we are used to all work and no play, we may be in for a big adjustment. Our goal should be to maintain a balance of work, play and service.

How long we enjoy retirement in good health is determined in part by *how* we live. We should apply good health practices to ourselves, not just to others. It's not too late to begin listening to the doctor.

Finally, well-being includes spiritual health. Our greatest retirement benefit comes from exercising our faith in daily prayer and in regular worship and fellowship with others.

A healthy faith in Jesus Christ as our personal Savior assures us of a permanent retirement in heaven!

It's time to feather your nest the right way. His!

PRAYER FOCUS: *Freedom to plan ahead is a blessing. Thank God for it daily.*

IN A WORD–VOLUNTEER

SCRIPTURE FOCUS

John 13:12-17
2 Corinthians 9:6-15

We all know women like Anne Erickson Allen. Anne helped establish a church in Plattsburgh, New York, more than thirty years ago. Since then, she's served on the altar guild, held leadership roles in the women's group, and been a member of the church council. She also has cut, sewed, and tied over a hundred quilts for charity and knitted hundreds of articles for children and nursing home residents. Anne also teaches English to refugees. I used to say, "Where do people like Anne find the time?" Secretly, I thought, "Who'd want to?"

For the last thirty years my husband and family have been the sole project I've needed to keep busy. Besides, sometime during my childhood Mother took me to a meeting of the Ladies' Aid Society, where I instantly determined I didn't want to earn a gold watch crocheting dish cloths!

Now that I am alone and I am drawing closer to God, I have discovered that a caring/sharing attitude has nothing to do with marital status or childish misconceptions. When I asked Him to "Create in me a clean heart," (Ps. 51:10) one of the rewards has been to understand completely what Anne meant when she said, "I don't think about rewards for my work, but in serving, they come."

According to a national poll, eighty million Americans are active volunteers. They are not just souls with little else to do. Robert Wuthnow, author of *Acts of Compassion,* writes that volunteers are highly individualistic and clear about their own needs. "They value their personal freedom, believe in the efficacy of self-determination, strive hard to succeed, take care of themselves and pursue the comfortable life." He goes on to say: "The motive for caring may be purely altruistic, even a kind of basic human need."[14]

Helping others is more than basic, it's biblical. Our Lord said, "I . . . have washed your feet, you also ought to wash one another's feet. For I have given you an example . . ." (John 13:14–15), and, ". . . whoever desires to become great among you shall be your servant" (Mark 10:43).

Many volunteer organizations screen applicants for characteristics common to Christians—caring, openness, self-reliance, tolerance and responsibility.

Helping others in His name glorifies Him and is an active expression of our deep gratitude for what He has already done for us.

In addition to spiritual benefits, service to others is good for our health, both emotionally and physically.

A study of 1,500 women involved in volunteer work revealed the following: 52 percent reported a sense of calm and freedom from stress after helping others; 44 percent said they felt stronger and more energetic and 13 percent reported fewer aches and pains.

The opportunities awaiting volunteers extend far beyond those in the days of crocheted dish cloths. In addition to the lengthy "We Need Help" lists posted in church offices, senior centers, and hospitals, helping others has taken on new significance.

Volunteers are pressed into service now as an immediate solution to our nation's social problems: homelessness, AIDS, job losses, and illiteracy.

A ten-word letter to the editor from Bob Klug, food and shelter programs manager of the North County Interfaith Council appeared in last night's paper. It read: "What restores my faith amid the doom and gloom? Volunteers."

I have been called and chosen. I want to live to serve and to serve and live. Do you hear His voice?

PRAYER FOCUS: *May the Master say of me, ". . . Well done, good and faithful servant"! (Matt. 25:21a).*

I knew I was solidly in touch with myself and in tune with God when He presented the opportunity for me to share His power and I took it!

I have a dear friend with whom I seldom have a leisurely visit. When she called and asked me to put on the kettle, I sensed more than tea was brewing—maybe a wedding.

I quickly set out my best china, microwaved two Weight Watchers apple crisps, then giggled to myself as I slipped the desserts onto over-sized candy compotes. Prim, reserved Shirley would be surprised at my silliness, maybe embarrassed. Her call made me feel special and I wanted to celebrate that feeling. She'd feel more comfortable celebrating the Reformation!

We met years ago when her husband joined the lay staff at church. We've seen our sons marry and helped one another sew seed pearls on our daughters' wedding gowns. Their youngest, Katie, is a Christian day school teacher and lives with them.

The moment Shirley sat down at my kitchen table, she blurted out, "Katie is pregnant."

Totally stunned, I could scarcely draw a breath. Anguish gripped my heart. I hugged Shirley through my tears. She sat rigid as if carved in stone. Her voice betrayed no more clue to her grief than when she called for tea.

"I'm numb," she said. "I feel like a bug, squashed flat. Tony and I were awake all night. If I could cry, for what would I cry? For Katie and for her ruined career? For what she's given away and can never reclaim? I'm devastated. She's disappointed us, the family, our friends. She's lied to God and she's lied to us, by professing a faith she doesn't live up to."

I wept for my friend who doubted her own worth as a Christian role model. I understood. It wasn't long ago that she sat across this same table and wept for me as I doubted my worth. Failed expectations hurt deeply.

I reached for Shirley's hand. "You know God's love for us is unconditional. He is *our* role model. We all sin daily. Katie's sin is just more visible. Remember, she is repentant and she isn't lying brain-dead in a hospital."

Her quick smile encouraged me to continue. "This is a Reformation celebration, after all. Martin Luther daringly reminded the world, as well as each of us, that it's faith, not good works, that opens the gates of heaven. And God promises to guide you, step by step, with the difficult decisions ahead—just as He guides me, when I listen."

Many of our sisters in Christ desperately need a caring listener to help them through a personal hurdle or family crisis. *Stephen Ministries* offers Christian lay people the training necessary to become effective "helpers." If your church does not already have a *Stephen Ministries* program, ask your pastor to inquire by contacting *Stephen Ministries*, 8016 Dale, St. Louis, MO 63117-1449 (314) 645-5511.

PRAYER FOCUS: *Dear Savior, comfort me and all hurting parents with the assurance that our heartaches and disappointments in those we love are expected in a sinful world. Thank You for Your unconditional love that helps us pick up the pieces and step forward to find the perfect love of eternity. Amen.*

I walked the last few steps to my front porch as bone-weary as I have ever felt. I don't know which made me the most tired—knocking on every door in my precinct or enthusiastically repeating my "Dannemeyer for U.S. Senate" sales pitch over and over until I lost my voice.

No matter, I thought to myself a few minutes later when my feet were propped up in front of a roaring fire. It is worth it. One-to-one contact is the most effective way to tell others about a candidate.

Politicians know what it takes to win an election. Mass media is vital in getting the candidate and issues before the public. However it is the foot soldier, the precinct worker, who gets the candidate's supporters to the polls on Election Day.

I read over my party's checklist. Today I completed house calls on the registered voters in my neighborhood precinct, about one hundred in all. By every name on my precinct list I penciled a 1, 2, 3, or 4. A "1" equals strong support for my candidate. A "2" indicates probable support—voter needs more information on what the candidate can do for him or her. A "3" means undecided. A "4" equals strong support for the opposition or the citizen elects not to exercise the right to vote.

Next, I highlighted the 2's and 3's. I will take those voters more literature about my candidate's promises and try to gain a commitment. A few days before election, I will leave "remember to vote" hangers on the doors of those voters interested in supporting my candidate.

Election Day will be dedicated to poll watching. By mid-afternoon I plan to telephone those supporters in my precinct who have not voted.

It sounds like a tremendous amount of effort, doesn't it? It is. Our nation is in crisis. We are in danger of losing our freedoms under a flag that promises, "One nation, under God, with liberty and justice for all." We must elect men and women who will restore Christian values at all levels of government. If we do not step up to protect our future now, next Election Day may be too late!

I put down the campaign guidelines and reached for my Bible. I don't know the date of my "election"—the day I will stand alone before God. I will be judged on one issue, my commitment to Jesus Christ as my personal Savior.

God's campaign plan is for those of us who believe in Him to go and " . . . make disciples of all the nations" (Matt. 28:19).

In my zeal to rally around Christ, am I willing to commit time and effort to call on one hundred neighbors, sharing the promise of salvation with each one? Am I willing to revisit the 2's and 3's with tracts explaining God's stand on issues affecting our daily lives?

Many of our forefathers died in the faith for the freedoms we now enjoy. Praise God, I have been asked only to *live* for Him. Do I commit myself fully? God knows my voting record. My neighbors know the truth—and I do, too.

How committed are you to campaigning for Jesus Christ and for Christian candidates?

Call the campaign headquarters of a Christian candidate you wish to support. Volunteer to help in your precinct. Praise God for the opportunity to meet like-minded neighbors.

PRAYER FOCUS:
Lord of the nations, thus to Thee our country we commend. Be Thou her Refuge and her Trust, her everlasting Friend.[15]
> —John R. Wreford, 1837
> "Lord, While For All Mankind We Pray"

THE NOT-SO-GOLDEN YEARS

SCRIPTURE FOCUS

Psalm 4:8
Romans 8:38-39

Everything went as planned. I found the empty suitcase in the garage. Then I let myself in through the family room door and hurried to the master bedroom where I opened the suitcase on the bed.

I moved quickly to the dresser. Laughter floated through the sliding glass door from the kitchen deck above. Margaret and her caregiver were having lunch.

The top dresser drawer opened to my touch. It was filled with neatly folded panties. Margaret's name was newly printed in indelible ink on the waistband of each pair. How many should I take? I had to decide.

I couldn't.

I opened the next drawer. Socks, each marked. How many of which colors should I pack? I couldn't think. I heard Margaret's child-like laughter followed by giddy gibberish she alone understands. Margaret is fifty-seven years old and her general health is excellent.

I turned to the closet. Which knit pantsuits would best stand the Alzheimer care center's dryers? Shifts are easier for toileting. Margaret no longer remembers when or how to go. Nightgowns? She sleeps an hour a night, paces the rest. Her husband is exhausted—mentally, physically, and emotionally.

I left the closet empty-handed. I had shopped for everything in Margaret's wardrobe. I had dressed and undressed my friend countless times during the last few years. I packed this same suitcase for Margaret as recently as a year ago for a weekend away with her husband and a few friends. The weekend was a disaster.

I stared at the suitcase. Margaret would not think me a friend today. I was violating her space—removing her personal things and taking them out of her home—forever.

With tears in my eyes, I began filling the suitcase. My heart was heavier than the bulging contents of the bag. "I will not leave you nor forsake you," God promised Margaret in Joshua 1:5.

A plaque hung on the wall. It was presented to Margaret six years ago when she retired after thirty-five years of faithful service as our church organist. Should I include it? No. She doesn't recognize it. Pictures of her children as babies? Yes, sometimes.

Within an hour, everything was in its place in her new room. She was in the locked ward of the twenty-four-hour Alzheimer's care center. Margaret has no way of knowing it is the finest facility in our area.

Margaret also has no way of knowing how fortunate she is to have a husband able to provide her with quality care, at least for awhile. Like most of us, his finances cannot survive the price tag of long-term care forever. Medicare doesn't cover nursing homes.

As women who live alone, we *must* face the prospect of developing a lingering, disabling illness requiring long-term health care.

Blessedly, more than one hundred insurance companies now offer long-term care insurance. The United Seniors Health Cooperative, a nonprofit consumer organization, suggests a policy that:

- Is guaranteed renewable.
- Provides an option to keep up with inflation by adjusting the amount the policy will pay per day of nursing home care.
- Covers skilled, intermediate and custodial care, with options for home health care, adult day care and respite care.
- Does not require skilled care before paying for custodial—or a nursing home stay before paying for home care.
- Covers physical *and* cognitive impairments.

To make my years *more* golden, I'm purchasing a policy while I am in good health, and before the cost increases with my age.

PRAYER FOCUS: *"I will carry you! I have made, and I will bear; Even I will* *carry, and will deliver you" (Isaiah 46:4b).*

THE REASON FOR THE SEASON

SCRIPTURE FOCUS

Psalm 86:12
Luke 2:1–20

Tears welled up and trickled down my cheeks. My hand quivered as I hung the last ornament on the first Christmas tree I had ever chosen, hauled home, carried up the stairs, and decorated–alone.

Just then, the telephone rang. It was Jane, the matron-of-honor at my wedding more than a quarter-century ago.

"Turn on the outside lights. I'm on the way over." Her voice bubbled with holiday cheer.

I greeted Jane with a forced smile and fresh makeup covering the red splotches on my face.

"You look terrible," she grinned, giving me a hug as she thrust a beautifully-wrapped package into my hand. "Go ahead and open it," she prodded.

"Two tickets to the Christmas Cantata?" I questioned. "We're not music lovers."

Her tone was glib, but her message was serious. "You and your husband weren't music lovers, but *you* might be. We both might be, if we change our focus. Let's think of it as an evening of worship."

"I know 'Jesus is the reason for the season.' But the family traditions that surround Christmas are powerful reminders of the way things were. For instance, most of our tree ornaments were gathered, one at a time, from places we had visited together," I told Jane as she poured each of us a cup of tea.

Jane sympathized, "The first round of holidays is going to be tough. They are for every woman learning to live alone again."

I looked at Jane. Were her eyes moist? Jane had ended her years alone with a happy second marriage!

She caught my questioning look. "I'm fine. Your pain rekindles some old feelings. If I had to go through holidays by myself again, I would treat them differently."

"I'm listening," I said, picking up my tea cup.

"Accept that holidays will be difficult. The ones like Christmas with the most traditions may never be easy, unless you break tradition and begin new ones."

"That's why the tickets to the cantata?"

She nodded. "And next year we'll have a tree trimming party, inviting guests to bring a special ornament for your tree."

"Or, I could ask my grandchildren to go shopping with me to choose new ones. The outing and tree trimming could become a tradition."

"You're getting the idea," Jane smiled. "I changed our family gift opening from Christmas Eve to Christmas Day. To fill in the empty spot, I invite neighbors for a Christmas Eve potluck, followed by attendance at the 11:00 P.M. candlelight service."

I ventured tentatively, "I've always wanted to invite someone from my church who is alone to come home for Christmas dinner or take poinsettias to our shut-ins."

Jane winked approvingly. I was learning as she had, that sharing Christ at Christmas is the one tradition that will bring gifts of peace and joy forever.

If you want to know His peace, be loving and caring. Show another woman living alone the true meaning of Christmas and help her light up the season again.

PRAYER FOCUS:
Angels, from the realms of glory,
Wing your flight o'er all the earth:
Ye who sang creation's story,
Now proclaim Messiah's birth:
Come and worship, come and worship,
Worship Christ, the newborn King.[16]
—James Montgomery, 1816
"Angels From the Realms of Glory"

My daughter's wedding reception was winding down. I headed for an empty table in a quiet corner, dropped onto a chair, and inched my swollen feet out of my new shoes. I opened my purse discreetly to count the number of thank-you notes and checks left to distribute. I found an extra envelope addressed to me.

The note inside read, "To Mom. Thank you for helping to make this the most beautiful day—perfect in every way. I love you. This certificate is for a one-hour body massage by Camille—I know you feel like you need it!"

The body massage was wonderful! So much so that I accepted Camille's invitation to join a group of women on an outing to Glen Ivy Hot Springs for a day of relaxation in the warm, mineral water pools. I tried a Swedish massage, a eucalyptus blanket wrap and as a finale, I really let loose and slipped into the mineral mud pool for a relaxing wallow.

Alyse's wedding was ten years ago. I have long ago forgotten the sensation of silky clay tightening my skin and eucalyptus oil cleansing my pores. However, I often recall the warmth that flooded through my body as I read my daughter's thoughtful note.

Thoughtfulness is a soothing balm that penetrates deeply into tired, bruised egos and regenerates the spirit. Christ taught us that thoughtfulness is a ministry of its own when He told us that whatever we do for the least of His brothers we do for Him (Matt. 25:40).

You and I may feel tired or bruised during the first days of being alone and be unwilling to step into the spotlight of an active social ministry. We soon learn, however, that we help our own healing when we think of others first. A "quick note ministry" answers the needs of both the sender and the receiver.

Here is a list of some people who would love to be on the receiving end of a quick note, or even a greeting card purchased at the store.

- *Someone you appreciate.* Remember the math teacher who taught you how to figure the savings on a sale item or the science teacher who helped you overcome your fear of spiders? Send a short note of appreciation.

- *Someone estranged.* Sometimes, in learning to live alone, we slip away from an even keel. If a relationship has cooled, due to miscommunication, a sharp word, or misunderstanding, send a short note asking and extending forgiveness. Put friendship above hurt feelings.

- *Someone who is ill.* Instead of writing "let me know if I can help," suggest that you are available to pick up a few groceries, stop at the cleaners or balance a checkbook. Even the arrival of a cheery get-well wish will help fill an empty day.

- *Someone who grieves.* We who have walked this lonely path know the importance of kind words and pleasant memories put to paper and sent with love. Suggest a date for a picnic or a walk in the park.
- *Someone who is a shut-in.* Those isolated from the mainstream of daily life are the most appreciative recipients of thoughtful notes. A pretty picture and large print help bring into focus the beauty of your caring. Tuck in a few jumbo snapshots of important people and places and bring the world a little closer to the heart of a shut-in.

Begin your "quick note ministry" by tucking an "I appreciate you" note in your minister's Bible when he isn't looking. Send articles to friends whose names or interests are featured in newspapers or magazines. Write yourself a note–tape a copy of your favorite upbeat Bible verse to the bathroom mirror. Be creative—add to this list and feel good!

PRAYER FOCUS: *Remind me, dearest Jesus, of my value as Your ambassador when I reach out to others with words of caring, concern and comfort. Let the joy of my ministry be reflected in a closer walk with You.*

A LITTLE SOMETHING OF OURSELVES

SCRIPTURE FOCUS

Proverbs 11:25
2 Corinthians 9:11

It all started when I asked Nancy for gift suggestions for my grandchildren. "It's hard for grandmothers to know what to buy for today's computer-age youngsters. And checks are too impersonal."

"Christmas is going to be different this year," announced my daughter-in-law. "We held a family council meeting and decided that *something of ourselves*—time, talent, treasures—should be woven into every gift. And you have unusual experiences that only you can share."

The whole family agreed to try Nancy's suggestion. Christmas hasn't been so thoroughly and joyfully planned in years. We didn't buy gifts, we gave them. I found that I had a wealth of ideas, and because I was alone, I had a greater latitude in the ways I could express myself in sharing.

A retired English teacher, I have always loved Shakespeare's plays. My gifts to teenage grandchildren were Sunday afternoon matinee tickets to "The Merchant of Venice," followed by a dessert/critique at my place. Afterward, one of the boys remarked, "Gee, Grandmother, I think of you as my 'homemade cookie and yeast roll' grandma. I didn't know you could talk about things."

I offered to drive an eighth grader to Saturday morning Morse code classes and ended up taking the course, too! I visited a mushroom farm, zoo, and art museum as a "grandparent helper."

Twice a month I take a granddaughter to piano lessons. It's a time for us to share and a gift of free time for her harried mother. My real gift of love—I opened my twenty-five year collection of *National Geographic* magazines to the scissors of elementary school authors.

Some of my most rewarding moments have been as a hospital auxiliary Pink Lady, so I looked forward to sponsoring fifteen-year-old Becky's membership in the Candystripers. Not long after, she dropped by in her starched, pink and white pinafore—my own teenage candy cane.

Her eyes danced as she spoke. "Thanks for opening the hospital doors to me. I've surely learned what responsibility means, and patience, especially with older people." She gave me a hug and added, "People talk about caring, but it's all talk, isn't it, Grandma, until they start sharing something of themselves?"

I brushed aside a tear. Pretty meaningful dialogue with a grandmother who just graduated from a "homemade cookies and yeast roll" reputation.

It's time to make a Christmas list of your loved ones. Beside each name write a gift idea that expresses something of yourself. Don't expect to complete the list in one sitting. Let the ideas blossom.

PRAYER FOCUS: *Thank you, Lord, for sharing the greatest Christmas gift of*

*all—the gift of Yourself. "For there is
born to you this day in the city of David
a Savior, who is Christ the Lord" (Luke
2:11).*

JOIN ME IN PRAISE

SCRIPTURE FOCUS

Psalm 95:6
Matthew 7:7-8

Women are joiners. And women who are alone again are particularly advised by well-meaning friends, neighbors, and clergy to "get out and join a club" as a cure-all for loneliness, depression, insomnia, muscle aches and nail-biting.

Our Chamber of Commerce maintains a list of local clubs and chapters of national organizations and their meeting times. Some club memberships are closely held to protect prestige and/or the standard of performance. Other organizations strive to *increase* their numbers for exactly the same reasons.

I found a unique group of organizations that play the alphabet game. Each uses an acronym to form the club's name, to announce its chartered purpose, and to attain the high visibility needed to attract a large following of like-minded zealots.

We all know MADD stands for *Mothers Against Drunk Drivers*, and that TOPS stands for *Take Off Pounds Sensibly*. What if Christian women, walking beside God, as we learn to live alone, banded together to establish an organization using the acronym PRAISE?

Our purpose would be to help other women who are alone experience full and complete lives, all leading to eternity in heaven. We would share the joy, peace and happiness we have through faith in Jesus Christ. The question is, can we find enough zealots to live according to the terms of membership?

P for Prayer—We believe in the dynamic and life-changing power of personal and corporate prayer. It is through a growing prayer life that we interact with our Lord and gain wisdom to live in a way that honors and glorifies Him (Eph. 6:18).

R for Rejoicing—We believe in gathering

together regularly to worship and praise our living Lord. Through His Word and sacraments we obtain everything necessary for living (Heb. 10:22–25).

A for Action—We believe in an active and involved life of discipleship. As disciples of Jesus Christ, we follow His example. We spend time with others teaching and living God's love in order to bring the Gospel into their lives, that the Great Commission may be fulfilled (Matt. 28:18–20).

I for Inreach—We believe in a caring ministry to one another. We accept that each of us, and every other woman living alone, is created in His image and deserves to be treated with dignity and respect. To this end we are committed to a caring ministry that enables our members to handle the challenges of life and to share God's love with one another (Gal. 6:10).

S for Study—We believe that the Word of God is our Lord's perfect revelation of Himself and His desires for our walk with Him. We are committed to daily contact with His

Word, which is essential to growth for every member in our spiritual family (2 Tim. 3:16).

E for Expansion–We believe in evangelism, personally accepting the challenge of our Lord to bring His message of grace and forgiveness to the world (2 Cor.12:9).

Please join me in PRAISE. Meet with your pastor. Suggest a PRAISE club within your church. Together we can reach out to the growing number of women alone, bringing the joy of His PRAISE into their lives.

PRAYER FOCUS:
Praise God, from whom all blessings
flow;
Praise Him all creatures here below;
Praise Him above, ye heav'nly host:
Praise Father, Son, and Holy Ghost.[17]
　　　　　　–Thomas Ken, 1695
　　　　"Praise God, from Whom All
　　　　　　Blessings Flow"

CHALLENGES UNSEEN BY OTHERS

SCRIPTURE FOCUS

Psalm 89:15
Psalm 100

Night has become a peaceful thing. The glow of the moon deepens. Flirtatious stars wink through the thickening clouds, lighting the way to eternity. A first snowflake, like no other ever before or after, dances to earth and silently kisses the shimmer of silver on the pond. The wind whispers its prayers through the stand of pines. Winter is like an angel smiling in the snow.

Truthfully, some of us began our walk together happy to be widowed or divorced. The white horse of our childhood dreams somehow carried our Prince Charming elsewhere. However, for most of us, the glass slipper—shattered by age or by stress—produced a painful break.

The brittle starkness of last winter's landscape still exists for some. But not for us. Our faith, rooted in Christ and led by Him, has been transformed into a journey of spiritual growth. We stepped out in faith to walk beside God.

God brought us to a new spring, planting tender shoots of confidence in us through His promise of answered prayer. We grew to accept our uniqueness in His image in a summer filled with the eternal beauty of his Beatitudes.

Autumn's gold added a rich tone to our inner beauty as we reached out to harvest and serve others in His name. And we continue to live in the harvest of His Word.

Our steps as newly single women continue beside the Master's. Spurred by our need and motivated by God's love for us, we are responding to the needs of others in all the conventional ways. But this winter's first frost may open our eyes to challenges unseen by others. Being alone, we may be sensitive to special needs crying for *our* attention. Let me illustrate.

Harold and Mary Ann, longtime members of Faith Church, divorced recently. Lonely and hurting, both desperately need and want to continue to be nurtured within the body of Sunday worshippers. Impossible in a congregation with only one service and one Bible study? It needn't be.

I share the theme of this book with other women whenever I have the opportunity. I am constantly reassured of its value and as often reminded of another common need. Too often I've heard the whispered plea: "Please include words of comfort and encouragement for those of us who are married, but feel alone. We are trapped in loneliness." How can we respond? How can our church minister to these Christian sisters? God wants us to reach out.

What about ministering to ourselves? God promises us an abundant life. No matter how spiritual a woman living alone may be, she sometimes feels shortchanged in the joy department. When people care for us our burdens lift, and as our joy multiplies we can share with others.

God's Word says to love your neighbor (Matt.19:19). He knows our need for human relationships. Does your church have a social ministry for mature singles? Brighten your horizon through an evening at the theater or accepting transportation and group seating at a ball game or concert. Group restaurant-hopping is fun. So is a mystery weekend on the bus–destination unknown! Would you like to spearhead such a ministry?

Albert Schweitzer was about our age when he addressed these words to a group of young people: "I do not know what your destiny will be. Some of you will perhaps occupy remarkable positions. Perhaps some of you will become famous by your pens, or as artists. But I know one thing: the only ones among you who will be really happy are those who have sought and found how to serve."[18]

Amen!

PRAYER FOCUS: *May the Lord bless and keep you in His peace forever.*

Notes

1. Frank B Minirth, M.D. and Paul D. Meier, M.D., *Happiness is a Choice* (Baker, 1978).
2. T.S. Eliot, "Portrait of a Lady," 1917.
3. Holmes and Rahe, "Special Readjustment Rating Scale", Reprinted with permission from *Journal of Psychosomatic Research* (Pergamon Press Ltd. Oxford, England.), 11, no. 2, 1967, 213-218.
4. John Ellerton, "Savior, Again to thy Dear Name We Raise," 1866.
5. June Masters Bacher. Unpublished work. Used by permission.
6. John Fawcett, "Blest Be the Tie That Binds," 1772.
7. Helen Taylor, "Bless This House." Boosey and Hawk, N.Y. 1927. Used by permission.
8. Abraham Lincoln, "Gettysburg Address." 19 November 1863.
9. Joseph Scriven, "What a Friend We Have in Jesus," 1865.

10. Oswald Chambers, *My Utmost for His Highest*, "The Purpose of Prayer" (Oswald Chamber Publications Association, Ltd., 1985).

11. "Soothing Rituals," *Victoria*, June 1991, 40.

12. Emily Dickenson, "Letter written to Abiah Root," *Letters of Emily Dickenson, Volume 1* (Harvard Univ. Press), 89.

13. Francis C. Key, "Before the Lord We Bow," 1832.

14. Robert Wuthnow, *Acts of Compassion* (Princeton Univ. Press, 1991).

15. John R. Wreford, "Lord, While for All Mankind We Pray," 1837.

16. James Montgomery, "Angels from the Realms of Glory," 1816.

17. Ken Thomas, "Praise God, from Whom All Blessings Flow," 1695.

18. Albert Schweitzer, speech in England, 1936. Taken from *Reader's Digest*, April 1951.

About the Author

Arlene Cook, divorced and "living alone," is a former elementary school teacher. She is currently Assistant to the President of Shuster Oil and Chemical.

She is an award-winning author (1982 Writer Digest National Grand Prize), and has published seven books, including *Love's Destiny*, *Forever Yours*, and *One True Love*, published by Harvest House.

From the Ashes of Hell, Creation House, released in 1973, was her first published book.

Her interests include real estate, travel, the stock market, her rose garden, and her grandchildren.

A lifelong resident of Escondido, CA, she is a member of the Grace Lutheran Church (Missouri Synod), which was founded by her grandparents.

She has 3 adult children Alan, Alyse, and Jon.